Beyond the Terrestrial!

(The Odyssey of Self-Resurrection)

Learn the Art of Spiritualizing Your Mind and the Heart!

Rimaletta Ray, Ph.D.

Copyright © 2019 by Dr. Rimaletta Ray.

ISBN   Softcover   978-1-950580-22-4

All rights reserved. No part of this book may be reproduced or transmitted in any form or by any means, electronic or mechanical, including photocopying, recording, or by any information storage and retrieval system without express written permission from the author, except in the case of brief quotations embodied in critical reviews and certain other non-commercial uses permitted by copyright law.

Printed in the United States of America.

To order additional copies of this book, contact:
Bookwhip
1-855-339-3589
https://www.bookwhip.com

For the Reader to First Consider

The Inspirational Geology of Self-Ecology

Make the Life from Berth
Your Heaven on Earth!

Let's reprogram our brains without vanity from Religiousness to true Spirituality!

Self-Resurrection is the reflection of the reality in a unique, technologically-enhanced, personally-processed way.

God in His Digital Form is Becoming Our New Uniform!

Your Inner Oasis is the Soul's Basis!
To Be Happy and Serene, Keep it Clean!

"They Tried to Bury Us, but
They didn't Know that We are Seeds."

(The Mexican wisdom)

1. Live with an Educated Zest - New Life is Abreast!

The book *"Beyond the Terrestrial !"* completes the series of five books on Self-Creation - *the spiral of the personality growth* on the path of Self-Resurrection in life. It presents the final, *Universal Stage of Self-Resurrection* – **SELF-SALVATION** or *Inner Maturity* - the core of our spirituality.

Life in its Universal Form is Our Eternal Uniform!

The Holistic Self-Actualization Pyramid / Books, featuring these stages:

5. Universal level	Self-Salvation	" Beyond the Terrestrial!"
4. Spiritual level	Self-Realization	" Self-Taming!"
3. Mental level	Self-Installation	" Living Intelligence or the Art of Becoming!"
2. Emotional level	Self-Monitoring	" Soul-Refining!'
1. Physical level	Self-Awareness	" I Am Free to Be the Best of Me!"

There are a lot of books on the market about different ways of accomplishing success, making more money, and obtaining spirituality on a various religious basis, but the most important aspect of self-growth and true spirituality, inseparable with it, remains untouched in its *objective, scientifically-verified, and digitally-enhanced holistic essence.*

Only then we can turn from an Object of programming by the mass media and the society into the Subject, programming himself!

We are on the path of a new evolutionary development that is now digitally-reinforced with new knowledge to an exponential level, and we must use it *as a trampoline for a new, holistically-channeled self-renovation and self-resurrection* in five main dimensions of life: *physical, emotional, mental, spiritual, and universal* at least at the dilettante level. There is an urgent need for our students of any career choice to get rid of the dead knowledge in their brains and embrace the breakthroughs of new knowledge with *the plan of action in the brain how to do it* in a simple, digestible way. We need a clear-cut, objective vision of dealing with life beyond survive!

To Self-Excel, Be the Best Version of Yourself!

Having the holistic vision of *a strategic self-growth* will help us build up the inner reformation image in a much more definite way. Order establishes the balance for self-confidence and the realization of self-growth in sync with the outside exponentially-changing life phenomena that we need *to perceive in the objective,* not subjective way. Albert Einstein once said,

"I need to know what God thinks; the rest is details!"

2. Self-Evolution is breaking through Knowledge Pollution

I tried to follow Einstein's principle in all my books that I want to be read and *inspirationally-digested* not as written by a certain Dr. Ray, but as the bits of my *personally- processed objective wisdom.* It is meant to help young minds find their own **ARIANDNE THREAD** *to escape the Labyrinth* of their society-imposed and self-negligence generated confusion and the pressure of common immorality of the **INNER MINOTAUR**, the beast that a Greek hero Theseus slew. He then found the way out of the Labyrinth with the help of the thread, tied by Princess Ariadne to the exit of the labyrinth.

Knowledge is power when it is properly generalized, selected, and stored!

The new times demand a holistic approach in providing the guidance or putting the Ariadne thread of Self-Actualization in the hands of young people to equip them with the **BLUE-PRINT OF SELF-INSTALLATION** in life. With it in mind, they are better able *to embrace the mind-to-mind and heart-to-heart* **LIFE–DIPLOMACY** of no obstinacy. To hit this very challenging goal, we need to promote the **RENOVATION OF INTELLIGENCE** and the formation of the new **SELF-MANAGENT SKILLS** in our education. There is an urgent necessity to tailor our young, life-entering minds to store in the brain the information files consciously so they could form a new, objectively- installed,

SELF-AWARENESS and **LIFE-AWARENESS** in sync.

We need *to put the Form + Content of life to thrive, not just to survive*! The objective Know-How discoveries of many excellent present-day thinkers, such as ***Drunvalo Melchezedeck***, *(the Mer-ka-bah structure of life),* ***Dr. John Hagelin*** *(the structure of consciousness),* ***Dr. Mandelbrot*** *(the fractal structures of Nature),* ***Dr. Merzenich*** *(the neuroplasticity of the brain),* ***Daniel Goldman*** *(Emotional Intelligence)* ***Bill Gates and Steve Jobs*** *(the digitized social structure),* ***Elon Musk*** *(the use of free energy and the probing of Space),* and many more forward-thinking scientists and technology geniuses do this work.

Unfortunately, ignorance is still ruling the world and *the superficiality of knowledge*, obtained by the students thanks to technological means is appalling! They need to be guided through the avalanche of information with a clear-cut goal in mind to make themselves better, more productive people. Quoting ***Dr. Bruce Lipton***, an informational biologist, *"We Need to Change the Biology of Our Beliefs" and Sculpture Ourselves Differently without any IFs!* ***We should help our cells live and create us in balance with the Universal Intelligence.***

To Life-Thrive, Become a Co-Creator of Your Life!

3. "No Soul is Left Behind!" *(Edgar Cayce)*

The process of **SELF-RENOVATION** is urgent, and no soul should be left behind in it because *"bad habits have a good tendency; either we kill them, or they kill us."* (Albert Einstein). I dedicate every word that my heart and mind generate in sync to my incredible son and to all those who were killed or died timelessly and whose souls went **BEYOND THE TERRESTRIAL** to come back again *in the unanswerable when.*

My son, ***Alexey Gazarkh,*** a very handsome, intelligent and noble man was killed in Ukraine last year by ignorant, hate-inflamed people just because he was a very successful businessman of the Russian-Jewish origin. I raised him as the man of ***a great soul, strong spiritual integrity, and personal charisma,*** but his very bright life had been timelessly stopped by hate that is ruling the Ukrainian society now. Alexey's soul went ***beyond the terrestrial boundaries*** together with my endless love and the thankful memory to God for the gift of his life that had enlightened mine and many of those who knew him - his family, friends and business associates world-wide.

I hope that our young generation will acquire the **LIVING INTELLIGENCE** that my book are all about to go beyond the terrestrially-conditioned bad habits, racial and national prejudices, limited self-consciousness, and most importantly, ignorance that is still *"the worst enemy of the humility."*(Albert Einstein)

The world is not becoming better, and it is getting bitter!

I dedicate this book to the open-minded people, able to resist the inner bitterness and self-pity and fearlessly explore the breath-taking future of the impossible, The souls of our loved ones go beyond the terrestrial space, somewhere out there and watch us from the Above, and we, as living beings, are supposed to clear up our souls and ***raise ourselves gratefully beyond the terrestrial turmoil.***

With the book *"Beyond the Terrestrial!"* I am trying to add a bit of my soul light to the common flame of the people who have the capacity to transcend any life challenges **and *go beyond the physical, emotional, mental, spiritual, and universal domains*** into the vastness of our unbelievable celestial future. The ancient people believed that the sky was the symbol of unity. They believed that when people were looking at the stars, even if they were very far from each other, ***they were united in their hearts and minds.*** I hope these pages will help you reason out life better for a conscious and successful **SELF-SURRECTION.**

Prefer Flying to Common Dying!

To Raise a Son is the Mission to Be Done!

I have completed mine
In the spiritual twine,
And I am proud of my son
That was the Only and the One!

"If there is any substitute for love, it's the memory."
(Joseph Brodsky)

Auto-Induction:
Don't Take Life for Granted; it's God-Granted!

4. The Power of Life is Beyond Survive!

(An Inspirational Booster)

The power of life
Is beyond survive!

    To establish the Universal Link,
    Put the heart and the mind in synch!

Make your heart feel,
And the mind perceive

    The power of IS
    In its revealing bliss!

Plug into the void inside you,
Feel the sacredness of IS,

    Learn the Power of NOW
    And appreciate life AS IS!

Don't Be Life-Negligent; Be Life-Intelligent!

5. Always the First!

I have very many successful stories to tell you about the impact that my *Auto-Suggestive Psychology of Self-Ecology* has had on my students, but one of them is the story about my fatherless grandson from Ukraine, my spiritual disciple.

In the awful situation of hate, a year before my son was killed, Alex insisted that his son Mark, *a teenager of 14* then, go to study to Israel. after Mark won the competition for the best school kids in Kiev that was organized by the Jewish organization Sakhnut in 2016. The boy with a Ukrainian mother, and a father that was only half - Jewish was accepted and had to leave his family and friends and study alone in Israel in the language and the culture that were totally foreign to him. *Mark was fearful, weak, wimpy, and needy*. On top of that, his father was killed in Ukraine after a month of his staying in Israel. I started working a lot with him on Skype, training him in English and telling him about *Steve Jobs, Elon Musk*, and the newest developments in science. I was inducting his young mind with self- confidence, will-power, and the determination to make it there.

Auto-Induction: ***In my life quest, I am the best!***

A month ago, **Mark Gazarkh** won a black belt in Dzudo and *a gold medal of the champion of Israel* in his age group. He is 17 now. When he called me, he said, " I kept repeating your inspirational boosters and the prayer that put my mind and the heart in synch: *"God is at My Right Side, Christ is at My Left Side, Light is Inside. Light is My Might!"*

I Can Roam Any Terrain with God in My Vein!

Nothing is Impossible

If You Make Your Inner Change Irreversible!

Add Your Bit to the Universal Outfit!

To Experience Self-Salvation, Put Your Life to More Consideration!

The Process of Self-Revelation is in the NOW Formation!

Don't Bury Your Exceptionality in Life's Banality!

6. Enjoy Your Life While You Are Alive!

*Life is a Continuing Battle
in Style,
Face it with a Smile!
Marvel at the Grander of All
And Knowingly Self-Install!*

The world is full of grey lives and unhappy people that are seeking to satisfy their internal hunger for self-realization and attain the stability of the desired equilibrium, but they don't know how. This book is the fifth objective step on the journey of knowing how to inspire yourself to be the Best You Can in the life's outcome.

**Your Heaven from Birth is on Earth,
Not Under It, or Up-Forth!**

7. Epigraph –
Life is the Choice of Having a Personal Voice!

The Process of Self-Revelation is in the Now Formation!

"I am not waiting for the future to happen; I consciously make it!"

(Alexander Litvin)

Learn to Fly in Your Mind and Be One of a Kind!

Contents:

For the Reader to First Consider – Make the Life from Berth Your Heaven on Earth!

1. *Live with an Educated Zest – New Life is Abreast!* ------------------------- Pages 3-14
2. *Self-Evolution is Breaking through Knowledge Pollution!*
3. *"No Soul is Left Behind!"*
4. *The Power of Life is Beyond Survive!*
5. *Always the First!*
6. *Enjoy Your Life While Yu are Alive!*
7. *Epigraph- Life is the Choice of Having a Personal Voice!*

Book Rationale - The Universal Level of Life is Our Guide! ----------------- Pages 20-35

(The Rejuvenation of the Soul is our Universal Goal!)

1. *We Yet Live in Dissonance with the Universal Consonance!* *(An Inspirational Booster)*
2. *Holistically-Strategize Your Digital Life Device!*
3. *Self-Growth is Multidimensional.!*
4. *<u>The Holistic Paradigm of Self-Actualization</u>*
5. *There is No System without the Structure!*
6. *A New Sense of Identity*
7. *A New Matrix of the World's Formation*
8. *The Rebirth of Self-Worth* *(An Inspirational Booster)*
9. *Centuries of Our Self-Formation in Transformation!*
10. *The Society needs a new Conceptual Literacy."*
11. *To Experience Self-Salvation, Put Your Life to More Consideration!*
12. *Join the Club of the Reformed Thinkers' Rehab!*

Introduction - "Go Beyond, Fully Beyond, Completely Beyond!" ------- Pages 36-49

(Aware Attention to Life Must be Earned at This Site!)

1. *The Psycho-Culture is in Self-Structure!*
2. *Self-Induction is the Short-Cut to Self-Production!*
3. *The Voltage of My Spirit is High and Infinite!*
4. *<u>Human Fractals Frame Our Spiritual Domain!</u>*
5. *Your Life's Goal is to Make Yourself Whole!*
6. *<u>Geology of Self-Ecology</u>*
7. *Spiritual Evolution is the Solution!*
8. *Enjoy the Bliss of the Uncatchable IS!*
9. *We are Guests on the Earth. So, Be Your own Boss!*
10. *"Nothing is Good or Bad, But Thinking Makes It"*
11. *To Life-Thrive, Become the Thinker of Your Life!*

Part One – Self-Identification and Our Digital Reformation ------------ Pages 50-64

(The Auto-Suggestive Psychology of Self-Ecology!)

1. *Our Terrestrial Form in the Year 2019 and on!*
2. *The Universe is Digital!*
3. *Our Evolutionary Objective*
4. *Acquire Emotional Intelligence with Diligence!*
5. *Digitally-Enhanced Universal Transformation*

6. *The Divine Will is Ruling us All Still!*
7. *" Mind over Matter" is Our Universal Strata!*
8. *<u>Our Salvation is the Holistic Self-Actualization!</u>*
9. *"Organisms are Algorithms."*
10. *The Ultimate Result Vision of Your Life's Provision.*
11. *Don't Put Your Life in Recess; Be Life-Obsessed!*

Part Two - " Wisdom Outweighs Any Wealth!"---------------------------------- Pages 65-77

Grains of Me and My Inspirational Philosophy)

1. *Self-Perfection is the Way to Self- Resurrection!*
2. *Your Main Obligation is Yourself!*
3. *Self-Attune to Life without Any Strife!*
4. *<u>Have a Clear-Cut Vision of the Self-Growth Provision!</u>*
5. *We Are of the Fivefold Life Bind!*
6. *Our Consciousness Integration is the Way to Salvation!*
7. *Spirituality is the Blood of the Universe!*
8. *Be Wise! Rationalize Your Self- Reforming Device!*
9. *Soul Renaissance is in Language-Speech Consonance!*
10. *<u>Internalize Your Emotions and Externalize the Mind; Be One of a Kind!</u>*
11. *Be Always Able to Say without Any Dismay!*

Part Three – Five Cycles of Being--------------------------------------- Pages 78-85

(Introduction to the Main Parts of the book)

1. *Focus Your Seeing on Five Cycles of Being!*
2. *<u>Our Salvation is in the Spiritual Maturation!</u>*
3. *Commit to Being Body + Spirit + Mind Fit!*
4. *Auto-Suggestive Phycology of Self-Ecology!*

Cycle One – Capture the Essence of Being!----------------------- Pages 86-115

*(The Cycles of Living - Mini Level- **Physical Dimension** - **Creation** - *Self-Awareness*)*

1. *I Do Not Need to Justify Myself!*
2. *To Soul-Refine, Envision the Holistic Life Paradigm!*
3. *<u>Self-Awareness – What is it in Evidence?</u>*
4. *I Am a Homo Sapience! (An Inspirational Booster)*
5. *A Whole and Life-Adjusted You.*
6. *Magnetize, Don't Demagnetize Your Soul-Device!*
7. *Keep Your Soul Intact from Any Evil Act!*
8. *Your Immortal Soul needs Conscious Control!*
9. *Learn to Thrive in the Four Elements of Life!*
10. *<u>Auto-Suggestive Meditation is Pivotal in Self-Formation</u>*
11. *Be a Cosmic Strategist! (An Inspirational Booster*
12. *Stop Being a Dope!(An Inspirational Booster)*
13. *Don't Just Survive; Be in Love with Life!*
14. *Be Also a Sage; Manage Your Age! (An Inspirational Booster)*
15. *I Have Set the Limit! !(An Inspirational Booster)*
16. *<u>Observe the Fractal Unanimity of Your Soul's Infinity!</u>*
17. *Have Enough Dignity to Protect Your Hygienic Unity!*
18. *Develop Alert Life Awareness!*

Cycle Two – Dissonance - *The Cycles of Living*------------------------ **Pages 116-147**

*(Meta Level - **Emotional Dimension** – **Maintenance** - Self-Monitoring*

1. *The Steering Wheel is in Your Spirit Still!*
2. *We Develop when We Train.*
3. *Constant Dissonance Destroys Us in Mass! (An Inspirational Booster)*
4. *To Be Inspired, Be Self-Inspiring!*
5. *Don't Be Stiff; Get Rid of the Negative "If"!*
6. *To Be More Life-Fit, Snap out of It!*
7. *Don't Be Self-Whining; Be Self-Redefining!*
8. *Self-Reformism Results in Personal Magnetism!*
9. *The Threefold Cord is Our Emotional Forte!*
10. *Commit to Being Soul-Fit!*
11. *Don't Let Anyone Litter Your Consciousness!*
12. *Soul-Processing is Self-Reassessing!*
13. <u>*MAKE LOVE ECOLOGY YOUR PSYCHOLOGY!*</u>
14. *Love is Always an Equation! (An Inspirational Booster)*
15. *Love Equation Needs the Auto-Suggestive Invasion!*
16. *Learn the Main Love lesson – Every Burden is a Blessing!*
17. *Serving and Giving is the Basis of Good Living!*
18. *Develop Love-Intelligence without Negligence!*
19. *To Meet Someone Halfway without Any Dismay!*
20. *Don't Rationalize Love! (An Inspirational Booster)*
21. *Be Strong Enough to Admit- I'm Not Love -Fit!*
22. *Cleanse Your Space with the Vocabulary of Grace!*
23. *Get Aboard of the Sanctuary of God! (An Inspirational Booster)*

Cycle Three – Sanitize Your Mind! Be One of the Kind----------- **Pages 148-164**

*(Mezzo Level - **Mental Dimension** – **Intelligence Formation** - Self-Installation*

1. *Be the Station of Digital Reformation!*
2. *Consciousness of God is Our Universal fort!!*
3. *The Eternal Mind is One of the Kind!*
4. *Consciousness is Intelligence at Work*
5. <u>*Self-Education is Crucial for Self- Formation!*</u>
6. *Form a Brand-New Habit of Thinking!*
7. *God's Inking is in Our Insightful Thinking!*
8. *Don't Just Know; Be in the Know!*
9. *Wounds of Intelligence*
10. *Self-Revelation is Personal*
11. *Change the Level of Awareness with Fairness!*
12. *To Be Self-Proud, Become Self-Rebound!*
13. *Mind-to-Mind and a Heart -to-Heart*

Cycle Four –- Consonance / *The Cycles of Living*---------------------- **Pages 165-186**

*(Macro- Level - **Spiritual Dimension** – **Evolution** - Self-Realization*

1. <u>*Try to Live Less Virtually and More Spiritually!*</u>
2. *Your Life's Award is in the Spiritual Fort!*
3. *Christ's Consciousness*

4. *The Spiritual Glee Makes Us Free!*
5. *On the Path of Godliness*
6. *Raised Self- Consciousness Propels Us On-ward,*
7. *The Process of Spiritual Hygiene*
8. <u>*To Be on the God's Porch, Build up Your Own Inner Church!*</u>
9. *Souls do not Die; They Spiritually Survive!*
10. *Delete the Evil with Your Spiritual Upheaval! (An Inspirational Booster)*
11. *Don't Be Color-Blind; Be Color-Refined!*
12. *Give Your Brain a Conscious Reboot!*
13. *Make Your Spirit Rewire, Uplift, and Inspire!*
14. *Honor Yourself to Honor Others!*
15. *Be the Spiritual Station for Love Inspiration!*
16. *Be in the Sanctuary of God!*
17. *I Am Infinity in Action! (An Inspirational Booster)*

Cycle Five – Be a Human Angel! - The Cycles of Living----------------- Pages 187-201

(Super Level - The Universal Dimension – Dissolution - Self- Salvation

1. *Accept Your Life in its Entire Mass!*
2. *The Process of the Universal Hygiene*
3. *I am God, and God is Me! We Are in Unity!*
4. *Equip Your Life's Watch with the Digital Torch!*
5. *The Law of the Right Human Behavior*
6. *Fill Your Inner Soul's Cavity with the Personal Gravity!*
7. *Beware of the Common Conformity Wear!*
8. *If Imported, the Vices Can Still be Reverted!*
9. *As Years Go By…*
10. <u>*The Fractal Formation is in the Universal Indentation.*</u>
11. *The Way People treat You, God Does!*
12. *Believe God, Not Just in God!*
13. *Self- Blessing is Life Obsessing!*

<u>Conclusion of the Inductive Self-Infusion</u>------------------------------ Pages 202-215

The Universal Level of the Existing Life Fort is Overwhelmingly God!

1. <u>*Strategizing Your Life is a Determining Factor!*</u>
2. *Develop Yourself Holistically, Not Mystically!*
3. *Your Time is Limited!*
4. *The Music of Life (An Inspirational Booster)*
5. *Go Beyond the Terrestrial; Be Celestial! (An Inspirational Booster)*
6. *The State of Inner Bliss is Beyond Happiness!*
7. *Radiate Your Personal Stamina!*
8. *Be the Living Intelligence in Action!*
9. *To Rise Beyond the Skies, Be Overly Wise!*
10. <u>*The Final Invocation for the Soul's Reformation!*</u>

<u>Post Word</u> - "I Have a Dream!"*(Martha Luther King)*-------- Pages 216-220

Destiny Has the Way of Working Your Way!

(All the pictures of the rocks are authentic. The other pictures are also from my collection.)

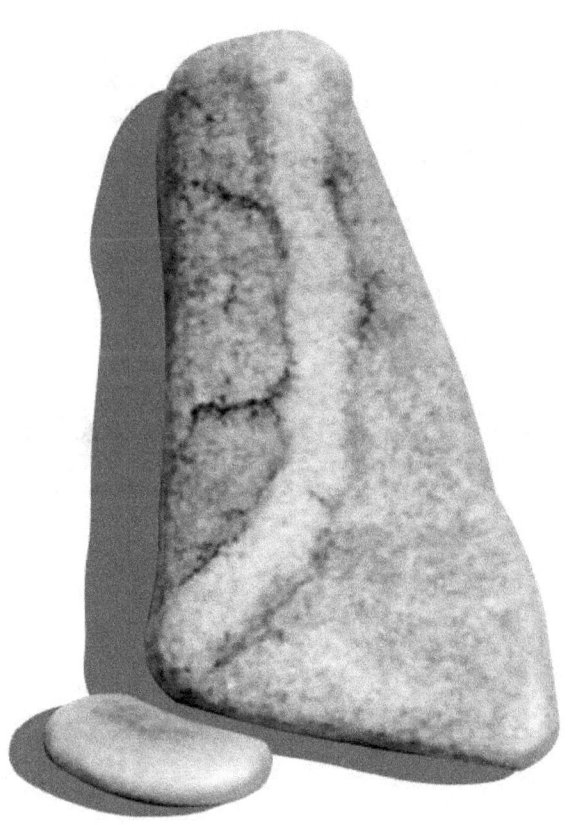

Help It without Any Dismay!

Self-Resurrection is a Personal Reflection of the New Reality Bay in a Technologically-Enhanced way.

Book Rationale

To Self-Excel, Live without the Society's Spell!

The Universal Level of Life is Our Guide!

(The Rejuvenation of the Soul is Our Universal Goal!)

"Time is Not Money, Time is Life!"

(Sadhguru)

**To Fit in the New Age Mold,
Be More Intelligent, Spiritual, and Very Bold!**

The Universal Level of Self Creation in Installation!

(A modern American sculptor - Benjamin Victor)

The Universal Consciousness is ruling the World; Be with It Aboard!

1. We Yet Live in Dissonance with the Universal Consonance!

We yet live in a dissonance
With the Universal Consonance!
Our Mer-ka-bah connection
Is in a prolonged retention!

To energize and revitalize
This celestial device,
We need to optimize
The ancient advice:
Make the heart smart and the mind kind;
Be one of a human kind!
Also, put your heart and mind in synch
With the God's approving wink!
Verify your every action
With the conscience's reaction!
Be alert, and if you have pricks that gnaw
Something must be in store!
Disregarding the voice of intuition
Reverses your life's mission!
Following it, though,
Helps you obtain the freedom to go

Away from the circumstances' burden
To a liberated action forum!

But we often have a conflict between the heart and the mind
In a personal, professional, or a romantic wind!
All we must do is to teach our guts
To go exponentially after the hearts!
Remember, reasoning in love
Won't kill the love stuff!
Thinking reasonably over any trouble
Will lower the consequences to double!

So, intellectualize your heart
And emotionalize the mind!
Expand your Mer-Ka-Bah wind,
And become One of a Kind!

To Inwardly Change,
Work Holistically on Your Mer-Ka-Bah Range!
(See "Flower of Life" by Drunvalo Melchizedek)

Individuate Your Digitally-Channeled Fate!

2. Holistically Strategize Your Digitized Life Device!

Our Salvation is in Self-Emancipation!

Live the life of your soul's sight,

not the one that others impose with their might!

"It's not enough to be the best. Be the Only! "

(Steve Jobs)

"Go Beyond, Fully Beyond, Completely Beyond!"

(The Tibetan Mantra)

3. Self-Growth is Multi-Dimensional

The book *"Beyond the Terrestrial"* is finalizing the conceptual structure of the *Holistic Paradigm of Self-Actualization*, that I see as the skeleton of our life's rout in its *physical, emotional, mental, spiritual, and universal make-up*. The concluding, fifth step of the *Auto-Suggestive Geology of Self-Ecology* is presenting the self-resurrection process in the Universal Dimension, featuring conclusively the stages of *Self-Awareness, Self-Monitoring, Self-Installation,* and *Self-Realization* and topping them with the **SELF-SALVATION**.

Life is going on, and it is objectively-Godly in its eternal structural form!

The previous levels are soul-exercising stages that are supposed to **HOLISTICALLY STRATERGIZE** your *mind + heart* maturation. This is *the process of self-emancipation* against religious dogmas, money limitations. people's ignorance and frustration! A soul-emancipated man beats the inertia of the society that distorts the beauty of life with materialism, indifference, impersonality, nationalism, racism, and other forms of a soul's death. *"The source of our wisdom is in experience; the source of our experience is in stupidity and lack of will-power."* (Carl Yung)

"Will your life More!" The will is your character's core!

This book presents the Universal Level of Self-Resurrection *in the holistically-integral manner,* taking you from one level of self-individualization to another one in a consistently-built conscious way, backing it up with inspirational mind-sets and boosters to fortify your spirit and raise your self-consciousness. A self-developing person builds up his / her *new sense of identity*, the identity of the one with *"spiritualized intelligence,"* considerably *raised self-consciousness,* and the synergy of **MIND + SPIRIT + HEART+ SELF-CONSCIOUSNESS+ SUPER-CONSCIOUSNESS!**

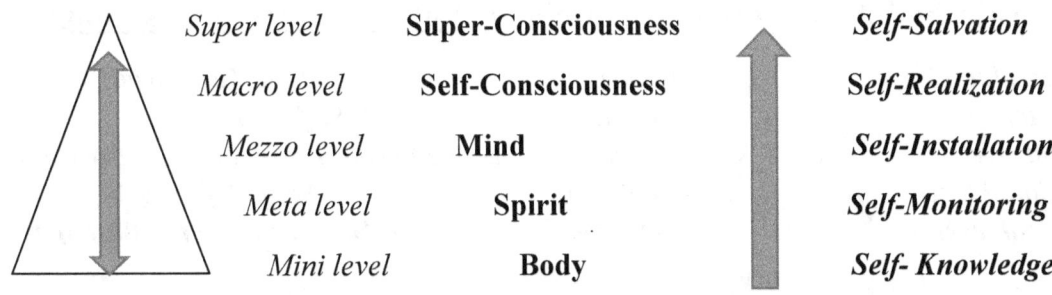

Super level	**Super-Consciousness**		*Self-Salvation*
Macro level	**Self-Consciousness**		*Self-Realization*
Mezzo level	**Mind**		*Self-Installation*
Meta level	**Spirit**		*Self-Monitoring*
Mini level	**Body**		*Self- Knowledge*

Body+ Spirit+ Mind + Self-Consciousness+ Universal Consciousness

==A Complete Individual - The Whole Self!

Self-Redefining is Soul-Refining!

4. The Holistic Paradigm of Self-Actualization

There are a lot of books on the market, addressing the problems of achieving recognition and success, material stability and self-confidence. There is also a lot of reference to the benefit of using affirmations and different quotations to help yourself on the path of self-transformation. However, the reading of these books, attending of all kinds of life-coaching seminars and webinars, and listening to numerous inspirational talks on You Tube might motivate us for some time, but this enthusiasm fades eventually because:

1) these books, seminars, talks, etc. *lack **the unity of the form and the content*** of the information presented; **2)** they do not provide ***a simple, actionable blueprint*** to follow; **3)** they do not ***appeal to the psyche*** of the one, interested in, what I call, ***Self-Resurrection*** that needs an instructional structure that helps a person stop being *an Object of the society's programming* and become a self-reliant and ***self-sculpturing Subject*** – a human being with the capital H.

This is where my books are coming to help you **HOLISTICALLY SCULPTURE YOURSELF** at the very unstable, digitally and intellectually challenging times that demand a lot of inspirational backing up for our physical survival and spiritual life-thriving, ***without any hostile imprinting!***

Don't be life-beaten, life-smitten, or life-paralyzed.

__Be Life-Mesmerized!__

All five books on Self-Creation are focused on ***the Inspirational Auto-Suggestive Psychology of Self Ecology.*** They are built consequentially in five levels that have never been presented so far in the holistic unity, but that are known in the ancient philosophy as – *mini, meta, mezzo, macro, and super* and that I call – ***physical, emotional, mental, spiritual, and universal.***

The Holistic Self-Actualization Pyramid / Books, featuring these stages:

Pyramid Level	Stage	Book
5. Universal level	Self-Salvation	" Beyond the Terrestrial!"
4. Spiritual level	Self-Realization	" Self-Taming!"
3. Mental level	Self-Installation	" Living Intelligence of the Art of Becoming!"
2. Emotional level	Self-Monitoring	" Soul-Refining!'
1. Physical level	Self-Awareness	" I Am Free to Be the Best of Me!"

Learn the Art of Holistically Spiritualizing Your Mind and the Heart!

5. There is No System Without the Structure!

1) Each book of *the Holistic Pyramid of Self-Actualization*, presented above, is built on the level above, starting with the book *"I Am Free to Be the Best of Me!* that initiates the *Self- Resurrection* process and shows how to move up in self-growth, starting with obtaining a scientifically-backed up *Self-Awareness (the physical dimension)*, learning further to conduct the emotional *Self-Monitoring (the emotional dimension)*, accomplishing the consciously-chosen professional *Self-Installation (the mental, educational dimension)*, attaining spiritual maturity and personal *Self-Realization (the spiritual dimension)*, and finally, holistically completing your mission in life through *Self-Salvation* that should be perceived not in conflict with any religion, but in a psychologically personable way at the time when *"the subject that is too profound for the human intellect"(Charles Darwin)* is being probed digitally.

The books are the matrix of a personality formation.

2) This route can be followed by you *from bottom to top and from top to bottom,* because each book consequentially retains the same five-dimensional structure, viewing each following stage from *the physical, emotional, mental, spiritual, and universal angles.* Each book can be read or studied randomly, too, if you need to *inspirationally boost your spirit* at any level.

3) Most importantly, each level of consequential and self-monitored **SELF-RESURRECTION** is presented in *small, a page long chunks of information*, specially simplified and conceptually-summarized, following the paradigm

Synthesis - Analysis - Synthesis!

4) The same structure is preserved after each chunk of information because *each page is crowned by the rhyming mind-set of an inspirational, finalizing character.* This paradigm is being consistently observed in every book and every part of them. The simplicity and the inspirational character of the text make every mind-set memorable and auto-suggestive in character. This feature is meant to help *up-load the information to a smart phone* and renew the memory bank for self-programming by way of self- help or **SELF-HYPNOSIS.**

5) The most useful feature of the book *" Beyond the Terrestrial !"* as well as of the previous four books of this series, is the fact that without any moralizing effect, you might get good food for thought, a great fortification of the spirit, and much material for the digitally-saved emotional back-up.

The Poetically-Shaped Word goes Better Inward!

6. A New Sense of Identity

The conceptual frame-work of all five books follows the structure of **the Russian Dolls,** Matryoshkas, when one level incorporates the next one, forming a ***simple, holistic system of Self-Installation in life***, The orderly structures of the holy books - **the Torah, the Bible, the Qur'an, the Tripitaka,** and others have the message for us that *life is terminal, and getting to heaven is the way of self-perfecting*, governed by our growing self-consciousness that is One with the Universal Consciousness of the Sun.

Be in a hurry to Self-Install; there is no lateness to the God's call!

The main concept of all the books that we need to instill in the mind more than ever are the words by a great Russian writer **Anton Chekov,**

" Squeeze the slave out of yourself – drop by drop!"

It means that an old sense of identity of a mortal, society-programmed, dependent, and constantly suffering human being should be substituted by ***a new sense of identity of an immortal, independent, spiritual being*** with the main goal of stopping to distort the reality and starting to co-create himself / herself to complete the evolutionary mission with the help of the digital means that expand our knowledge horizons exponentially now.

"A computer is the bicycle of the mind!"(Steve Jobs)

In other words, we need to bridge the gap between the initial dream of self-realization and the one that we become in reality. Life is phenomenally complex, and it is impossible to know it in its entirety, but it is essential for us ***to be a conscious part of the mind-boggling Universal immensity.*** Our essentially religious education and the eternal values that have been instilled in us, are being fortified now by new knowledge and science breakthroughs, speeding up our **SPIRITUAL MATURATION** that is our evolutionary goal.

<u>Just believing is not enough now. Knowing and feeling is what matters!</u>

By the way, when Nils Boor, a great German physicist, staying at the death bed of Albert Einstein, pleaded his dying friend to give him a sign if he believed in the existence of God in the Universal domain of life, probed by him, Einstein's last words were, ***"I don't believe,*** *(a long pause followed, giving Nils Boor food for his doubts, but then came a weak, but firm conclusion)* ***I know!"*** True believing is in knowing!

Knowing is Self-Determining!

7. A New Matrix of the World's Formation

A new level of information is changing the world, making us leave the old matrix of thinking, speaking, feeling, and acting behind. We are entering **THE NEW MATRIX** of the world's formation only through our transformation!

It is the stage at which we need to reason out **OUR NEW EXTRA-TERRESTRIAL GOALS.** We should stop fighting for our sincere religious beliefs and change our **SELF-KNOWLEDGE** and **LIFE AWARENESS** through new education because the religious evolution has been the stage for *our slow spiritual transformation for centuries.* Now, *the space + time speed* has technologically accelerated all the spheres of our life, but our own transformation is lagging obstinately behind. The point is, the difference between religiousness and spirituality is transformational, too. Sadhguru says,

"Religion is following the messenger, spirituality is following the message!"

We need to change our reasoning, our limited thinking, and prioritizing the money power in the economic evolution that is only secondary. New times generate new knowledge, new knowledge means new thinking, new thinking transforms us into new human beings, able *to go beyond the terrestrial boundaries into the mind-blowing celestial future!*

We are all One under the Common Sun!

We also need to stop blindly believing that God will change us because we are faithful and righteous and go to church every Sunday. We need to understand that all the revelations that are given to the humanity in holy books: *the Torah, the Bible, the Qur'an, the Tibetan Book of the Dead, the teachings of the Hare Krishna, the Yoga Sutras* and many other most insightful messages are focused on our **ONENESS** with the **ALMIGHTY GOD.** We know that, but we are not aware of that! The Qur'an (*Surah 13, yaat 12*) states that God does not change what happens to people, until people themselves change what they have in them.

We are all in the court of "the Most Gracious, Most Merciful, Almighty God."

So, the Universal Level of Self-Actualization in life is the level of a new life-awareness, the knowing about how to obtain *Self-Salvation* that the most enlightened and personable people among us impact us with. Then each of us will have the right to declare auto-suggestively,

I'm Drifting into the Reverie of a New, Intellectually-Spiritualized Me!

8. The Rebirth of Self-Worth

(An Inspirational Booster)

The rebirth of self-worth

Is the hardest job on Earth!

    You need to discover your identity

    And restore your lost innate dignity.

Your inner pride and personal magnetism

Should be charged with self-patriotism

    That demands constant self-respect

    Without a destroying self-pity speck!

Such job generates love for Self

In your every single cell!

    But self-love must not be side-tracked

    By being self-centered and full of whack!

The attitude of gratitude

Needs to become your new aptitude,

    And your free-range talking

    Must be restricted by the mind's blocking!

Also, you should never shade the Sun

For the loved ones or any talented one!

    Only then can you fly in your mind and shine

    Because such self-worth is always divine!

Self-Induction:

I'm Never at Rest; I'm on the Spiritual Quest!

9. Centuries of Self-Formation in Transformation

In sum, the book *"Beyond the Terrestrial!"* is the concluding chapter in *the Manuel of Life* for the young minds, hungry for knowledge and ready to give the world the best they have. It features the steps of *Self-Resurrection* in the **UNIVERSAL REALM** of life that we are heading to, making our Self-Salvation scientifically and religiously justified. For centuries, our religious and social programming has been pyramidal in structure. Therefore, we need to create *our own pyramidal paradigm of self-creation of a new, free human being.*

I am Free to be the Best of Me!

The system of books on the *Holistic Self-Actualization in five levels* is my modest attempt to create a simple, *inspirational instruction* to help young people develop their "*spiritualized intelligence*" and raise self-consciousness, presenting the scientifically backed-up mentality.

For centuries, we have been evolving *sporadically*, but at the time of an unprecedented digitizing of our disconnected. souls, *holistic personal growth* comes to the up-front of our evolution. I see the need for *a simplified instruction on life and living* in my students who hungrily up-load a lot of most inspirational boosters and mind-sets into their smart phones. The auto-inductive boosters resonate with them personally and serve as *the up-lifting hypnotherapy*, or **SELF-HYPNOSIS** that they resort to when their spirits sag.

Each page of every book provides a chance for more self-awareness.

Even though all the books are consequentially-connected into one **SELF-HELP BOOK**, you can choose to open any part of any book to perform the necessary **SELF-SCANNING** and **SELF-BOOSTING**. The books will provide the information needed to get back on the *individually-channeled track.* Thus, *the structural, educational, psychological, and inspirational aspects* of all five books come together and form a simple **MANUEL OF LIFE** at hand that we all need at the time of the digital soul-disconnection even on the religious plane.

Be aware of your joy and despair and uplift your spirit every minute!

We need to use this incredible evolutionary time to our absolute advantage. I hope that my five books will be one more step forward on this life-determining path. They are meant *to meet your self-help physical, emotional, mental spiritual, and universal needs spiritually.*

You are Free to Be the Best of Thee!

10. "The Society Needs a New Conceptual Literacy."

The words of Dr. B.A. Efimov above point to the urgent necessity to help our young people *conceptualize life in a new, much more advanced way.* Unfortunately, the self-consciousness of the young generation the world over is shaped now by the TV, digital gadgets, and the opinion of the crowd. Their future is being formed by the images of crime, vulgar sex, getting rich quick, virtual games, cooking expertise, and the ways of losing extra weight, as well as numerous images of twisted reality that they are being fed up digitally. In other words, young minds are being shaped by the **MASS MEDIA SOCIAL MATRIX** that is so powerful now that it is even over the President. I see an awful confusion in my students' eyes and the question: *How to live?*

Chaos is ruling the world, so what?

We are still at the top of the pyramid of intelligence and our evolutionary role is not to yield this place to robots, at least at the level of true love, morality and conscience, **based on <u>forward thinking and aware attention to life and living.</u>**

First, on top of an urgent necessity to develop our students critical thinking skills and their insightful individuality, there is a great need to teach them to speak, to converse, and to communicate **on the mind-to-mind** and **heart-to-heart basis**. We must teach them new Speaking Skills, Conversational Skills, and Interactive Skills. Globalization of education and business interaction must be based on *aware attention* to what is being said, listened to, and heard. Attention has become the main commodity in business on the Internet and to develop it for the **educational. professional,** and, most importantly, *personal* growth is a present-day must. The core of self-consciousness is the world of values that is determined by our being now, but it should be the other way around;

Our Consciousness should determine Our Being!

Otherwise, we'll be becoming more and more **disconnected on** *the physical, emotional, mental, spiritual, and Universal levels*. The gaps of self-knowledge and life awareness are widening as fast, as the exponentially growing technological progress. Beautiful words by Immanuel Kant come to mind here. Kant believed that there was "*a supreme principle of morality in the world*", and he referred to it as "*The Categorical Imperative.*" he wrote, **"Two things surprise me – the starry sky outside and the world of values inside us."**

Let's build up the Fences around Our Souls and Clean Our Corrupted Life Goals!

11. To Experience Self-Emancipation, Put Your Life to More Consideration!

(An Inspirational Booster)

On the cosmic plane of our universal mission,
We all fit for one life position!
    It's either life-beaten, life-smitten, life-paralyzed, or
        Life-mesmerized!
Most of us
Are life-beaten by our daily fuss;
    Many are life-smitten, some are life-paralyzed
    With troubles, drugs, alcohol, or any other pollution device.

I belong to the last group
That survives in the life-mesmerized loop!
    When life beats me, I resist!
    When life smitten me, I persist
In being mesmerized
With the grander before my eyes!

    I drop down my jaw
    When I see a splendidly made Pigou.
I say, "Wow!"
To Elon Musk's new space ship bow!
    I marvel at the Internet
    That is God-set

To unite us all as One
Into the Web Wide Clan!
      So we could appreciate our human-ness
      And beat down the animal-ness!

So, when you are life-beaten, take a minute to think
That you need to take a life-wonder drink.
      Open your mouth and breathe in
      The prana that cleanses your inner sin.
It'll help you get back
On the life-mesmerized track!
      It'll make you a beauty fan,
      And it'll prolong your life span!
   You'll lighten up your routine life
   And let it flourish and thrive!

Dear God!

Protect me from Me and those that don't follow Thee!

The number of mega churches is growing all over the world, but the humanity is getting worse.

Protect me from that course!

Self-Induction:

I Can Roam Any Terrain with God in My Vein!

12. Join the Club of the Reformed Thinkers' Rehab!

"I want to Desperately Live –
To Eternalize what Can Be Seen,
To Celebrate the Unforeseen,
To Humanize irreversible,
And to Realize the Impossible!"

(My translation form Alexander Block)

These wonderful words are in the mind and the heart of every one of us, However, the actions we take to realize our most beautiful dreams make us different from berth because we do not follow a simple rile:

Make Your Life from Berth the Heaven on Earth!

Here's a small anecdote:

- *"Doctor, will I die?"- " No doubt about it," said the doctor.*

We are all mortal, but what we leave behind and how content or discontent we are with the self-realization in life when we are dying is the question.

To go far, do not sleep at the wheel of your life's car!

Live without the Society' Spell; Be Yourself!

(End of Book Rationale)

Introduction
(The Auto-Suggestive Psychology of Self-Ecology)

"Go Beyond, Fully Beyond, Completely Beyond!"

Aware Attention to Life Must be Earned at this Site!

Let's Reprogram Our Brains Without Any Vanity from Religiousness to True Spirituality!

"To Follow the Universal Bliss, Stand in Awe to All That IS!

The Temple of God is in the Heart + Mind Walt!

1. <u>The Psycho-Culture is in Self-Structure!</u>

Auto-Suggestion is the Onto-Genesis of Self-Formation!

Our Salvation is in Self-Actualization!

Auto-Suggestion is the Onto-Genesis of Self-Formation!

Self-Resurrection has three paths to it:
  1) Praying (talking to God)
  2) Meditating (listening to God)
  3) Acting (following God!)

This book is about integrating the skills of new knowing with new living, feeling, thinking, and believing!

Self-Strategizing is Inspirationally-Energizing!

<u>Life-Making is in Action-Taking!</u>

2. Self-Induction is the Short-Cut to Self-Production!

My understanding of the **SELF-RESURRECTION** process goes beyond the religious or an accepted view that *life-coaching* can be learnt. I adhere to *Leo Vygotsky's* belief that it is *"a self-processed and self-learnt conscious action."*

Self-Induction: ***My life is going on, and it's beautiful in its every form!***

We need spiritual energy to love, to create, to walk, to work, to eat, to breathe and to talk. The inspirational boosters that continuously come out of my mind help me become tougher and more aware of life. I also use numerous rhyming inspirational mind-sets to boost your spirit and communicate the conceptual content of my ideas ***in simple, digestible way.*** It works better with my students.

Build up Your Forte with an Inspirational Word!

I write my prescriptions of joy to inspire them *"to fertilize their minds with thinking."* (*Albert. Einstein*) Surprisingly, my rhyming words break at the end of a sentence ***in a rap-like way***, adding a special rhythm to the concepts that they communicate. This is how I started writing them, and this is how they keep coming to me continuously, keeping me from being ever vexed and discontent with life.

The posture, a smile, and a good mood are my inspirational food!

My professional academic career has also proven to me that such ***inspirational, psychologically-backed up boosters*** do their transformational work for my students much better and much more insightfully self-help-wise than any neutral lecturing. According to a famous Russian parapsychologist, *Alexander. Litvin*, *"Life is the time for reasoning out the present and shaping the future.* ***I am not waiting for the future to happen. I consciously make it!"***

The new bio-medicine has it that our bio-energetic field is closely connected with the bio-energetic field of the Earth, and since the energy of the Earth is getting weaker due to the ecological pollution, our biological informational fields, that are inseparable from ***the Universal Informational Field***, get energy depleted, too. The spirit of self-reformation is getting weaker and weaker.

So, raising self-consciousness is instrumental because it is healing our common eternal human soul that each of us is a part of. It is possible only in unity of the ***body, spirit, mind, self-consciousness*** and ***Super-Consciousness*** - the symbiosis of the five essential ingredients of our ***spiritualized life fractals.***

Make "Joy-ology" Your Life's Psychology!

3. The Voltage of My Spirit is High and Infinite!

Having read, or at least looked through the previous four books, you have, no doubt, become *a much wiser Self-Actualizer.* The Universal Consciousness is ruling the world, and it is the outcome of your holistic self-growth, or *your inner maturity.* It is in your ability to connect to it, raising your self-consciousness, and accomplishing true *"spiritualized intelligence."* (Dr. F. Bell)

These are Five Main Road Signs for the God-Attuned Soul!

(Universal Consciousness / *Self Salvation*)

5. Self-Salvation — *Universal Dimension*

(Self-Consciousness / *Self-Realization*)

4. Self–Actualization — *Spiritual Dimension*

(Mind / *Self- Installation*)

3. Self-Fulfillment — *Mental Dimension*

(Spirit / *Self-Monitoring*)

2. Self-Control — *Emotional Dimension*

(Body / *Self- Awareness*)

1. Self-Revelation — *Physical Dimension*

The Glow of Light from Inside Creates Your Life!

I want to draw the parallel here between *the Holistic Pyramid of Self-Actualization* above and *the musical octave.* We are all familiar with the musical scale: do, ra, mi, fa, so, la, ti, do - 8 notes of an octave. *As science has it, the Universe is the system of musical octaves.* An octave is the common unit of eight musical sounds: A,B,C,D, E, F, G and then A again, *but of a higher pitch*.

The universal vibratory system determines the frequency of the musical notes that vibrate at a higher pitch at each new level, or with each new octave. *Our souls have the vibratory nature*, too, and therefore our self-creation, as part of the Universal process, repeats itself at a higher level and with a higher pitch if we consciously orchestrate our inner life on the Universal note grammar.

To Life-Thrive, Holistically Strategize Your Life!

4. Human Fractals Frame Our Spiritual Domain!

I have always tried to attune myself to the inner music of the people I communicate with, trying to be on the same vibratory level, if possible, and if I do not have to lower mine. The vibrations of the people that do not care about their ***inner sounding*** is always the lowest, and we normally have problems in the interaction with such people. ***Inner sounding is much more important for human interaction than a clicking in chemistry*** that dies out very soon as a flash of a spark without any soul-orchestrated connection. Obviously, the soul of each of us is a musical note of a certain pitch, and to be thriving in life, we need to heighten this pitch to the Mozart level each day. I have always considered myself to be ***the note La***. That's why I make myself happy and joyful with inner humming: ***La-la- la ! La-la- la! La- la- la !***

Our inner soul reflection and inner melody radiation is a complex melody that ***we should orchestrate ourselves.*** I have been playing ***Mozart, and Chopin*** on my inner piano all my life at the moments of elation. I hear ***Bach*** each time I am praying because his unearthly music connects us to the Divine. ***Vivaldi is*** in my soul when I am romantically-inclined. "The Moon Light Sonata" by ***Beethoven*** is framing my thinking, and the first symphony by ***Tchaikovsky*** is triumphing in my soul when I celebrate success in my dealings.

By analogy with the music in our souls, I consider the incredible discovery of ***Dr. Mandelbrot,*** mentioned above, about ***a beautiful fractal structure of nature*** to be a great chance for us to try and develop our own beautiful fractal structures since we are an integral part of the Mother Nature, too. *(See the previous books)*

The present-day technological evolution is integrating each life into ***holistically-developed*** **HUMAN FRACTALS.** Developing spiritually, ***we generate the inner beauty of incredible unity and balance,*** beautifying the world with our presence in it. I write about my observation on this evolutionary breakthrough in science in my book "***Self-Taming!***" that is featuring the previous, spiritual level of self-resurrection. It is never a stable upward process, but rather, the movement of the musical octaves from one pitch to another.

The Spiritual Fractals of Our Being:

Body + Spirit + Mind + Self-Consciousness + Universal Consciousness = The Spiritually-Refined You!

The Voltage of My Spirit is Strong and Infinite!

5. Your Life's Goal is to Make Yourself Whole!

As is indicated above, this book is a logical conclusion of the serial of my inspirational books, comprising the *Inspirational Geology of Self-Ecology.* It is presenting the process of self-installation and self-realization in five philosophical levels – **mini, meta, mezzo, macro, and super,** or in the *physical, emotional, mental, spiritual, and universal dimensions of life.* It is the last accord in my five-part inspirational symphony of **spiritual maturation.** Going beyond the terrestrial level signifies the Universal Level of self-creation beyond out terrestrial boundaries to unite with the celestial life.

The Holistic Route of Self-Resurrection:

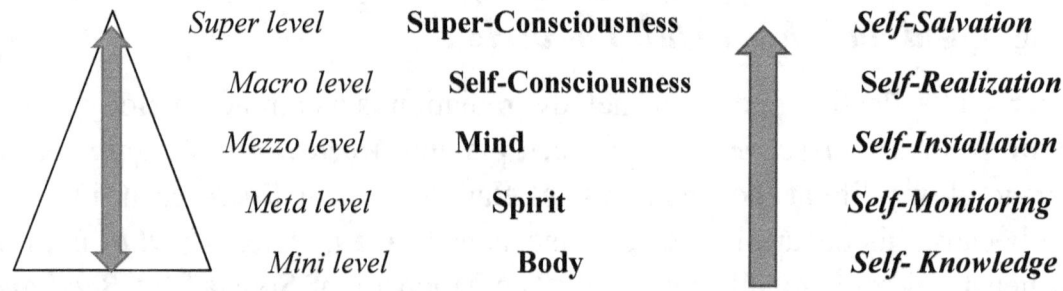

Body+ Spirit+ Mind + Self-Consciousness+ Universal Consciousness

==*A Complete Individual - The Whole Self!*

The spiritual maturation is a life-long process that is going on at the religious, educational, science-oriented and experiential levels. However, with most people, it is unconscious, sporadic, often monitored by the church priests and occasional praying at the time of despair. God, instead of a co-creative force, becomes the habit of stagnation. People go to church to revitalize their faith.

But the connection with God needs to be direct, without any mediation! The spiritual growth is our main path is life that evolves first, from *the world of Minerals to the world of Plants, then to the world of Animals, next to the world of People, topping the pyramid of evolution with* **the Universal Intelligence - God.** We are the nearest to God in our consciousness, and it is our primarily **personal duty** to be connected to *the Universal Mind* that brought us to life, to begin with. A person needs to take this duty consciously, raising his / her self-consciousness, enriching self-education, and establishing a firm unity of the **HEART+ SPIRIT+ MIND** *in all spheres of life,* not just in the church environment and during occasional good deeds done on an impulse, not in the unbreakable unity of **believing and knowing.** *(See Chunk 2 above)*

Conscious Living means Conscious Learning!

6. Geology of Self-Ecology

Five books on the of Self – Resurrection are my modest contribution to our on-growing process of spiritual maturation. Each book has its own auto-suggestive motto and together, they make up **the Geology of *Self-Ecology.***

The book, *" I Am Free to Be the Best of Me*," ascertains the main guide-lines on the path of gaining a solid **SELF-AWARENESS** and **LIFE-RATIONALIZATION.**

Auto-Induction: ***In my Life-Quest, I can be the Best!***

The book "***Soul Refining***" helps you become more skillful in your *emotional maintenance* to perform **SELF-MONITORING** consciously and consistently.

I Keep my emotions and the tongue in the captivity of the mind's run!

Putting your mental frame-work in shape and enriching it experientially in *ten most essential intelligences holistically* is being done during the professional **SELF-INSTALLATION,** or in the mental realm of life.

Auto-Induction: ***The Greatest Art of all is to Self-Install!***

Next, you are invited to round off the process of never-ending *spiritual maturation* by taming your bad patterns of behavior with **GRACE** with the help of the book "*Self-Taming!*"

Life-Gaining is in Self-Taming!

Next comes the most actionable and creative step in life when you individuate yourself and attain full **SELF-REALIZATION.** You need to govern your spiritual growth from top down, following the rule "*As it is Above, so it is below."*

Auto-Induction: ***I Consciously Infuse my Self-Realization Fuse!***

Finally, we acquire wisdom to *"Go Beyond the Terrestrial "* in the universal plane of life, by focusing integrally and consistently on each level of **SELF-SALVATION** holistically. I invite you to pursue the goal of self-installation in life on *the auto-suggestive, inspirationally-rhyming note.* You take yourself beyond the boundaries of common-sense life by assimilating the accumulated knowledge holistically to probe the puzzling enigma of life in the universe.

"Go beyond, Fully beyond, Completely beyond!"

Our Self-Salvation is in the Complete Self-Realization!

7. Spiritual Evolution is the Solution!

There are incredible breakthroughs in all fields of knowledge thanks to **THE TECHNOLOGICAL EVOLUTION**. Biology and Immunology have become the fields of knowledge that give rise to **Bio-Technology** when many other fields of knowledge get engaged.

Science is no longer separately rated; it's getting holistically-integrated!

Scientists are working on very compelling experiments with human genome, destroying certain genes, using crisper and generating new ones. Editing human embryos and doing other mind-boggling and most engaging manipulations with life, we reject the old, dead knowledge and head to the breath-taking horizons of the new one.

Self-Salvation is in Our Spiritual Maturation!

Now, if science is changing the inner design of life impersonally, why can't we do it through the **personal auto-suggestive ways**, perfecting our inner and outer life here and now.

Let's stop our knowledge-limited whines and

better our inner designs!

So, I am inspiring you to design your life, fantasizing about it, like **Isaak Asimov**, and conquering new highs with your *"creative imagination."(Carl Yung)* The self-creation process beyond the terrestrial boundaries is, in fact, *the ability to protect oneself against going down the rocky road of self-corrode.*

Each of us needs to auto-suggestively protect his / her bio-energy that is based on the personal Informational Field and its unique ecology in five dimensions of life consciously, continuously, and religiously.

We are heading toward an amazing future that we are shaping for ourselves, each one of us separately and unitedly! The purpose of such development can be well-inducted with:

I am No Longer Automatic; I am Spiritually Aristocratic!

My Life is Full of Bliss;

It Makes Me Stand in Awe to All that Is!

8. Enjoy the Bliss of the Uncatchable "IS!"

In Sum, we are all suggestible to some degree, and in this book, as in several others, I focus on developing our resistance to troubles and tribulations and bettering the inner spiritual content of our souls, too. *We all need a lot of inner boosting and inspiration as our main psychological tools of life.* They are vital when we often lose **alert awareness** and stop appreciating life "**AS IS.**" An injection of a rhyming mind-set that you might have stored in your memory will get directly to the emotional center in the brain, **AMYGDALA**, and it will give you *an uplifting shower of awareness and gratitude* that life is going on, and it is beautiful, no matter what.

Work on your conscious living - being, becoming, and perceiving!

Alert awareness can be constantly sharpened with the help of auto-suggestive work, or **SELF-HYPNOSIS**. We get better in synch with *"The Power of Now" (Eckhart Tolle)* and its unfathomable beauty. Having charged yourself with an inspiring word at the right time, you will quicker get back to the reality and continue taking life in stride. All the boosters in this book are meant to do just that. In fact, they act as a wake-up call to the mind and the heart. They can easily stay in the memory because **THEY RHYME IN THE MINDS TWINE.**

Intellectualize your heart and emotionalize your mind; Be One of a Kind!

The pictures of the rocks with the ***authentic imprints*** in them that are placed throughout the book, are the conceptual illustrations of my alert attention to life that I try to develop with every breathing moment, alongside with *the ability to read into different signs and meaningful coincidences* that happen all the time to help us adjust to life consciously.

"Turn your wounds into wisdom!" (Oprah Winfrey)

The rocks are randomly found by me at the ocean, and each time there are messages for me that I love to decipher. I cherish **the moments of revelation** when this or that image strikes me as recognizable and insightful, helping me resolve a problem that it might manifest. Nickolas Roerich, a great Russian artist and philosopher, the museum to whose artistic contribution respectfully opens its doors to the visitors from all over the world in the center of Manhattan, wrote, when he lived in India on the spiritual mountains of **Shamballa** that he most beautifully depicted in his art, *"The first thing that comes to my mind when I think about beauty is the Beauty of Thought."* It leads the Universe forward.

Nothing can Ever Beat the Magic of "SO BE IT!"

The Picks of Our Spiritual Horizon are in Self-Consciousness Rising!

Auto-Induction:

Beauty is Me; Beauty is My Philosophy!

9. You're a Guest on this Earth; So, Be Your Own Boss!

Concluding the introductory part of *the book series on Self-Resurrection*, please note that the auto-suggestive mind-sets at the bottom of each page are addressed to your **INNER SELF,** your personal exceptional growth, channeled by enriched self-awareness and conscious life-channeling. Start composing your own ones, try to respect *"the brevity of thought" Shakespearian rule* in their form and content. We are messed up with the avalanche of information flow, and the ability to select what you need is indispensable here. The rhyming word engages the mind just enough not to overload it with redundant information. Sadhguru says, *"How people are is their choice. How I am is my choice, no matter what they do, or say. No one can make me angry, happy, or unhappy.*

These privileges I have kept for myself."

You will soon see that it's no accident that the auto-suggestive psychologically-backing-up boosters have an inspirational impact on your psyche. It happens because ***they consciously maximize your life effort*** in focusing it on self–architecture and your will-power that both depend on your emotional make-up.

The ancient said, ***"Every house has its own mice under its roof."***

Putting it differently, every mind has its own patterns of behavior and bad habits, and it's the responsibility of its owner to clean the attic of the junk. Five books, presented in the holistic pyramid in **Book Rationale** are just my modest attempt to provide the plan of action for you to better yourself consciously in your attic.

If you read, studied, or ran your eyes through the previous four books, you have sculptured yourself in the physical dimension *(the book "I Am Fee to Be the Best of Me!"),* you have perfected yourself emotionally with the help of the book ***"Soul-Refining!"*** You've expanded your intellectual out-reach *(the book "**Living Intelligencer the Art of Becoming!**"),* and you are working on self-taming - the book *"**Self-Taming.**"* Your spiritualized intelligence wouldn't let the best version of you ever slide down to the worst version of you.

To Be Life-Potent, Become More Life-Content!

The book ***"Beyond the Terrestrial!"*** summarizes conceptually the five main steps of your **SPIRITUAL MATURATION** in *the physical, emotional, mental, spiritual, and universal dimensions.* If the collection of five books of which this book is the final one helps you structure your life in your own, individual way, my mission will be complete.

Inner Dignity is the Base of Our Personal Equity!

10. "Nothing is Good or Bad, but Thinking Makes It"

(William Shakespeare.).

Each one of our mental warts

Is the sum of our daily thoughts!

    Both brains are involved in processing the thought,

      But the question is into What?

The left brain is responsible for the structure;

The right one deals with the meaning's fracture.

    <u>*The brain is a perfect domain;*</u>

    <u>*We just need to fix the mind's main!*</u>

The questionable beliefs and habits

Need to be changed into new mind gadgets!

    The dome of the conscious mind

      Will help you to rewind

The pesky mental warts

Into constructive and creative thoughts!

    You will restructure the life's haze

    Into the harmony of the musical space!

Literally, our constructive thoughts

Orchestrate our inner worlds!

    Yes, I am getting old, I say, so what,

    Age is the most beautiful part of my world!

Thus, I never let Ignorant People's Dumbness

Litter my Growing Extra-Terrestrial Gladness!

11. To Life-Thrive, Become the Thinker of Your Life!

When the Mind + Spirit + Heart Link is Cultivated, Life Becomes Regulated!

**Inner Might is the Aristocracy of Your Spirit;
Make Yourself "Ageless and Timeless" in it!** *(D. Chopra)*

(End of the Introduction to the Holistic Self-Function)

Part One

Self-Identification

and

Our Digital Reformation

("From the Relative Truth to the Absolute Truth!")
(John Baines)

Living to the Full of Your Potential is Exponential!

In the outcome, an electric charge will be growing in the physical body, and it will change the spiritual aura of the mind. As the result, your self-sufficiency, self-reliance, and self-confidence will raise you to a new level of self-consciousness and Self-Resurrection.

Instill Order in Your Life to Thrive!

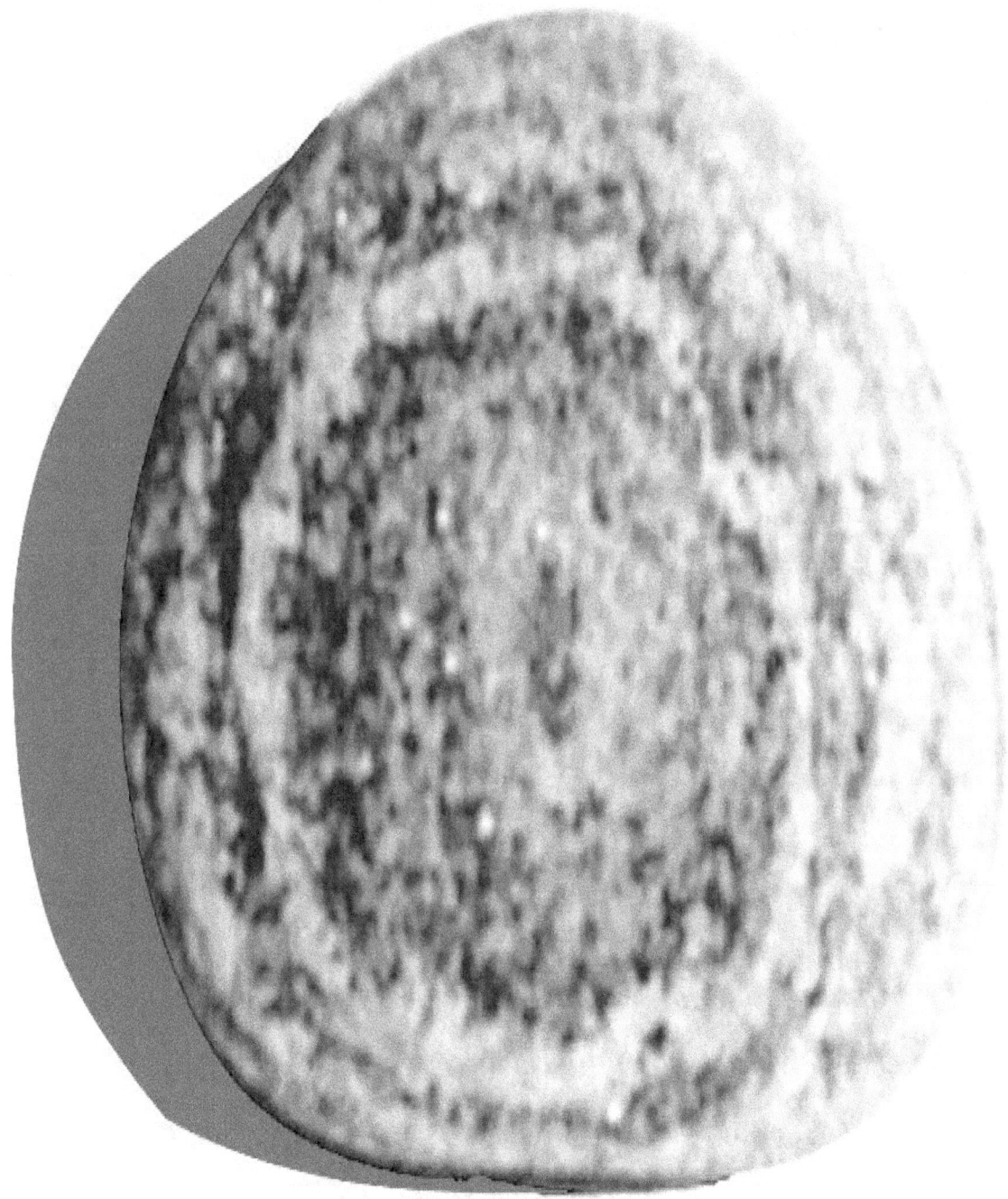

Chaos and order in their global expulsion are shaping our evolutionary function.

Big Bang in You is Going On, too!

1. Our Terrestrial Form in the Year 2019 and on!

Our terrestrial form

In the year 2019 and on

        Should undergo a celestial reform,

        Continuously going on and on!

We must use the God-given might

To enlighten our common terrestrial site!

        We need to let wisdom, love, and compassion

        Become our daily life's fashion

And to allow the unbeatable celestial light

To fill up our immortal souls' sight!

        Thus, we'll cleanse our polluted systems

        Of any evil insistence!

Then our lives in 2019 and on

Will fit peace and kindness uniform!

        With the celestial blessing,

        We'll sustain any global recessing!

We'll fill up our common world

With consciously-earned Godly reward,

        And we'll turn our terrestrial dissonance

        Into the Universal Consonance!

Finally, we'll become One

Under our Common Celestial Sun!

        I wish I could live then,

        in the unanswerable "WHEN?"

Be Wise! Digitally Strategize Your Spiritual Devise!

2. The Universe is Digital!

(An Inspirational Booster)

The greatest discovery of our time

Is that the Universe is digital, fine!

We revolutionize our knowledge

And enhance the intelligence.

We are learning to decipher the Master Brain

And intuit its mind's domain!

We call it God, and we refine

Our souls with the Universal Laws in twine!

The Universe is programming our life,

And we get aware of the true reality to thrive!

Being both a particle and a wave,

We're finally arriving at the Celestial Bay!

The auto-suggestive work and self-assessment can be more productive if you are always monitored by the holistic blueprint of self-transformation. Keep this paradigm engraved at the forefront of your mind and guide yourself by its fractal unity.

Body+ Spirit+ Mind + Self-Consciousness Universal Consciousness =
A New, Inwardly-Integrated Self!

It is very helpful for the never-ending intelligence enrichment *in the holistic mode of your general intelligence formation* and an exponential outlook expansion. Remember, the spiritual level goes after the mental one, and the universal intelligence cannot be tapped unless you qualify mentally for it.

Let's Be Immune to the Digital Mind's Inflation and Become a Conscious Human Nation!

3. Our Evolutionary Objective

Self-growth needs to be always self- monitored and self-reflective. It means that you must constantly **X-ray** *your thoughts, feelings, and actions though the grid of conscience.*(see the book "Self-Taming! - Spiritual level) Conscience is the **HEART + MIND** unity that generates a solid magnetic power both inside and outside of our being. It's our evolutionary objective to raise our consciousness and fill our hearts up with love. *This philosophy was introduced to the Earthlings by Jesus Christ as the* **REVOLUTIONARY WAY OF SELF-RESURRECTION.** *We know that, but we are not aware of that.*

We keep living in our heads, disregarding the heart, its intuitive perceptions, and the warnings of the numerous coincidences in life that the **UNIVERSAL CONSCIOUSNESS** is sending to us as the signs that we are supposed to decipher. ***This is what being self-aware + life-aware means.***

We need to be physically, emotionally, mentally, spiritually, and universally attuned to **THE UNIVERSAL IT** that the digital breakthroughs have revealed to us. It becomes clear that as the divine creatures of life, we cannot be surpassed because the most sensitive and perceptive electro-magnetic connection between us and the universe is our **CONSCIENCE.**

Conscience is our direct Digital Line with God!

No doubt, our evolutionary objective is to sharpen our perception of life universally via this unique spiritual device that can never be digitally reproduced.

The Fractals of Spiritualized Beings:

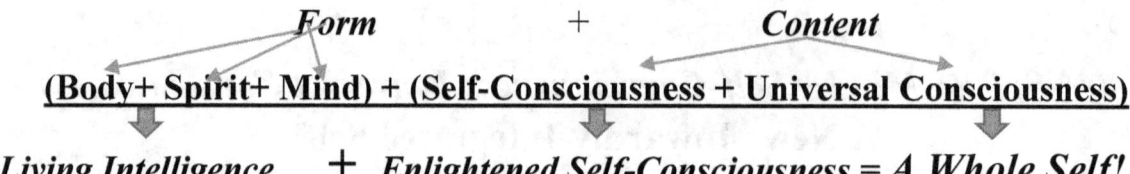

Form + *Content*

(Body+ Spirit+ Mind) + (Self-Consciousness + Universal Consciousness)

Living Intelligence + *Enlightened Self-Consciousness = A Whole Self!*

Self-consciousness, monitored by conscience can, of course, have spasms that we need to remove. Mark Twain called it **"sleepy conscience, and a person with** *it is useless on top of the ground; he ought to be under it, inspiring the cabbages."* Learn to consider the heart first. Listen to its rhythm, it's intuition, and its bio-energy-based state. ***That's your Fate!***

Switch Your Aware Attention from the Mind to the Heart
And Be Good at That!

4. Acquire Emotional Intelligence with Diligence!

To accomplish that, we need to train ourselves and our kids to control emotions in extreme situations, ***reject acting on impulse***, and think before saying something. These are the most vital skills of **LIVING INTELLIGENCE**. Our ability to appreciate the gift of life and help it prove its unique sense to us within the allotted time span is the core of the wisdom of life.

So, to clean of the inner scum, learn to be balanced and calm!

Life is the heart-focused electro-magnetic circle, energy-wise. The religious matrix that had been installed in us for centuries reminds us to follow the Divine Will and be guarded by the objective, godly truth -

"Be calm and know that I am God."

I would like to conclude thus chunk of information with ***the third basic auto-inductive rule*** that reminds us about the necessity to identify with God and perfect ourselves through loving each other and serving each other.

Every Human Contact is a Responsibility!

There is one most amazing thing about us humans. We are incredibly talented, creative, and boundlessly imaginative. The wonders that people have been creating for centuries and continue to create now are all breath-taking, but we take ***these pearls of our unbreakable unity of the mind and the heart*** that is at the core of any creation as a matter of course.

We grudge the words of sincere praise, recognition, and admiration for the smallest accomplishment done by a colleague, a friend and even a loved one because we keep comparing and envying that all these grains of genius were not in our heads and that the success that we are seeking hit someone else.

We are under-loved, under-appreciated, and under-rated!

Talking about our technological evolution, let's focus on our inner transformation not in word, but in action. ***Let's eliminate the most soul-degrading shows with aggressive fights and verbal abuse that are being cheered by the public,*** electrifying the performers with outrageous manners that are beyond any limits of decency. I shudder inwardly with the dirty sincerity of the godless public.

"Only beauty that is consciously perceived can save the world!" (N. Roerich)

Serving and Giving is at the Heart of Living!

5. Our Digitally-Enhanced Universal Transformation

(An Inspirational Booster)

Our evolutionary formation

Is going through digital transformation

From millennia of blindness

<u>To the renaissance of Christ's Consciousness!</u>

We are still obtaining the critical mass

Not to fall onto our ignorant ass!

We are still in search

Of our cultural porch,

Or have we lost the identity

Of our human integrity?

Can we all co-exist

In the global Web-Net mist?

For sure, we are becoming more international,

Rather than American, German, or just national.

I also try to make the most

Of what my luck does not roast!

I drift absent-mindedly

Into a New, digitally-enhanced Me!

My life experience validates

What the Bible rates

As a spiritual growth

Of the spiritually - ignorant moths.

But it is still an enigma
To my personal stigma!
Negative emotions still drag me back
Onto my aloof personal drama track;
I am not spiritually-transformed,
I am now more digitally-formed!

But I am on my way
To a new consciousness bay
Because our spiritual transformation
Remains to be in the Universal Mind's formation!
God makes us all digitally-international
Not white, yellow, black, or national!
We are all becoming One
In His celestial Tongue!
We may mean different things,
But the essence of our human wings
Takes us all to the God's digital domain
And makes us have the Universal Love Vein!

It's only with love that we can now digitally transform
Our yet imperfect spiritual uniform!

Make Life from Birth Your Heaven on Earth!

6. The Divine Will is Ruling Us Still!

As a human being, you have received the body and have been granted the material life of your soul in it. What you do with this life is up to you! Your body has gotten the mind to evolve it in every cell, so you could **complete your mission on the planet Earth in synch with the plan of the Universe!** Your personal intelligence, *or your personal computer,* is a part of the Universal Intelligence, or *the Master Mind*, and the more intelligent and connected to *the Universal Intelligence* you are, the higher you evolve on the ladder of evolutio*n* that, as science proves, is monitoring this process digitally.

Self-Evolution is in breaking through Self-Pollution!

To evolve is to objectively observe *the rules of the Above* in five dimensions: *physical, emotional, mental, spiritual, and universal* in the **UNIVERSAL SCHOOL OF LIFE** with the departments of **Godly Wisdom, Modern Science, Emotional Intelligence, Love Cultivating, Family Formation, Children Rearing, Career Building, Money Managing, Business Structuring**, etc.

To Self-Excel, Modify Yourself with Grace at every Life Phase!

If you were a diligent student in life-schooling, able to graduate from the school of life successfully, you'll have no regrets about the uselessly spent life time in it. Degrees do not matter here; the quality of the lived years is what makes a difference! According to *Albert Einstein,* **"Happiness is the space you are in and the time you are given in it."** What you make of your space and time is up to you! The choice is yours, but it depends on the intelligence you gain and the ways you choose to use it - to construct or to destruct your life, to give or to take, to love or to hate, to shine or to rot. Life has a different quality depending on **the state of our self-consciousness**, based on **the objective internal judgement** that generates pure, individual, godly wisdom.

To conquer the world, go consciously and tirelessly forward!

I suggest you instill in your consciousness the plan of action for Self- Resurrection in five, mentioned above dimensions, **holistically and not sporadically.** It will help you inspire and **MODIFY YOUR INNER SELF**, making your reality more motivational and electrifying your spirit on the path of attaining conscious self-realization in life. However, self-growth in all five stages should not be the imitation of anyone's life success, or a blind following of any one's subjective advice that we get in abundance on the Internet now.

You Must Individuate Your Way without Any Dismay!

7. "Mind Over Matter!" is Our Universal Strata!

The Earth needs fewer grey lives and much shinier, self-realized ones! Unfortunately, we have become **"a race of human robots"** *(David Icke)*, the race of programmed minds that live automatically, unconsciously, and irrationally.

The automatization of life feeds it up with self-strife!

Obviously, it is the holistic unity of the **body, spirit, the mind, and self-consciousness** that we must be working on the entire life, following the main scientific laws and re-programming our cells holistically and consciously. I have verified my paradigm with hundreds of students that got self-inspired and self-transformed with the vision of **the Holistic Paradigm of Self-Actualization,** installed in their minds and hearts. It changed their career and money-chasing goals into the **SELF-INSTALLATION STRATEGIC PLAN OF ACTION.** There is no postponing; action counts only Here and Now!

De-materialization of the Soul is our Common Goal!

Let me quote here a wonderful piece of wisdom, left for us by **Steve Jobs:**

"Don't raise your kids to be rich. Raise them to be happy!

Then, when they grow up, they will know the value of things, not just their price. The watch that costs only $30 dollars and the watch that is $300 dollars show the same time! If you drive a car for $30.000 or a car for $300.000, the road and the distance that you must cover will be the same. You'll come to the point of your destination, anyway!"

Whatever you think, say, feel and do in your life's ado, you present a physical, emotional, intellectual, spiritual, and universal copy of your Self-Guru!

So, let's de-materialize, emotionalize, intellectualize, spiritualize, and universalize our lives!

To Generate Consonance in the Life's Gutter,

Put Mind Over Matter!

8. Our Salvation is in the Holistic Self-Actualization!

The present-day times and the speed of our life-changing technological evolution are both *mesmerizing and very confusing*. Much confusion is, generated by the fear of losing the job and becoming useless and outdated. The skills of adjusting to the technological reality and *a new degree of perseverance and emotional stability* come to the forefront of life in the minds of those who are aware of what is going on the scene of adjusting to the new life.

To be part of the New Life's cell, everyone must digitally re-invent oneself!

It's easy to re-invent yourself when you are 20, but it's very hard to adjust to the fast-changing reality when you are 30, 40, 50, and older. *The old patterns of behavior and stereotypes of thinking are in the way,* and they must be broken and re-programmed in accordance with the new vision of the reality and, most importantly, with the new mental and emotional set-up in us.

The point is, many new professions will relate to our understanding of emotions. Even the electrical Tesla cars and all kinds of drones will be geared *to our emotional intelligence.* Information is the essential ingredient of our life, and the more information we accumulate and probe for its validity for us, the stronger our emotional make-up will be. *We need to absolutely learn to meditatively-relax!*

Our Emotional Adjusting needs Technological Fasting!

The future people will be able to go beyond their biological commuter make-up. We'll modify our bodies and minds with the help of the exponentially-growing **Biotechnology.** Eventually, *we'll become connected into* **one bio-technologically-wired global circuit,** and a skillful hacker might be able to break into our personal bio-computer and program or re-program it.

The development of the newest science **Neuro-Biology** is also at the pick of evolution. Soon it will become possible *to digitally put the mind and heart in sync* and manipulate human beings' decisions and actions.

Therefore, all my previous books, featuring the *physical, emotional, mental, and spiritual levels of Self-Actualization in life* are accentuating the urgent necessity for us to work on *the unity of the heart and the mind* to never lose the control over them.

In other words, we have the right and free will to change our present, but we have no right to modify the divine plan of the future.

"It's the Territory of God!" *(S.N. Lazarev)*

9. "Organisms are Algorithms!" *(U.N. Kharari)*

The present-day science is probing **the brain-mind link** that is broken at present and that is supposed to help us understand the essence of consciousness that is our **MAIN CREATOR,** the Master Computer, the Universal Intelligence that we all call God.

A modern Israeli historian, *U. N. Kharari* presents a new trend in science **Bio-Technology** that will be ruling our life in the future. He writes," *If we manage to de-cypher the algorithms of the brain, we'll be able to re-create ourselves."* Dr Kharari says that the technological evolution goes in three pivotal directions: **1) Bio-Engineering -** *the creation of new organisms and modification of the existing ones*. **2) Bionics** – *the combination of the organic and non-organic organisms, using nanobots - Nanotechnology* **3) And the most radical way** – *the creation of the non-organic forms of life.*

Dr. Kharari predicts that **the bio-technological revolution will change the balance between democracy and dictatorship**. He writes, *"We are heading toward digital dictatorship. A small group of people will be operating the humanity from one bio-technological center since people will be connected into one totally obedient army."*

Hopefully, the mind-boggling breakthroughs in science will help us understand what Universal Consciousness really is, not letting us forget about our organic nature that is **unbreakably connected to the Universal Intelligence** that bought us to life, to begin with. As we think, so we are!

"As it is Above, so it is below!" *(The Hermetic Rule of life)*

Unfortunately, most people remain fearful about the essence of their technologically-backed-up evolution. Obviously, <u>we need to go beyond these menacing predictions</u> and <u>humanize, not de-humanize our technological breakthroughs</u> to the point that it will become our best friend, not our ruling enemy.

Nothing is impossible if we make our human evolution irreversible!

I think that one thing will never be surmountable for the artificial intelligence. It is the ability of a human mind *to experience pricks of conscience* that is our intuitive sense of the right and wrong, or our ability to follow the **DIVINE WILL** and react objectively and with respect to It.

Let's Not Ban the God's Divine Plan!

The Time Imprint goes in Unison with the Universal It!

Life is Going on in Its Ever-Beautiful Form!

10. The Ultimate Result Vision of Your Life's Provision

There is an avalanche of information on zillions of sites about self-transformation, but most people, especially the young ones, do no process it consciously, chasing the money and fun sides of life as if they are rehearsing their lives or playing virtual games with it.

They have information on the subject, but they are unable to sort it out and make it practically applicable for themselves. It's not the matter of a smart book and motivation, it's the mater of the **PLAN OF ACTION** in the mind and the inspiration, installed in the mind and the heart to bring this plan to action!

<u>Living Intelligence needs to be holistically developed without negligence!</u>

To be successful in the mission of Self- Realization and Self-Resurrection in life, we need to have *the Ultimate Result Vision* (*the URV*) of the route we are taking, or A **PERSONAL LIFE GPS** in the mind. At the highest level, we need more life awareness and consciously-processed intelligence. It is everyone's personal business *to obtain digitally-enhanced wholeness of a spiritual being of the Universe.* (For more see the book"" Living Intelligence or the Art of Becoming!)

The Holistic Paradigm of Self-Resurrection:

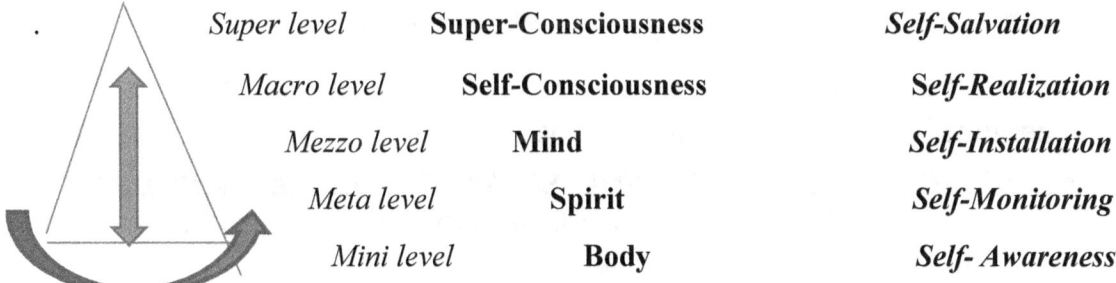

Super level	**Super-Consciousness**	*Self-Salvation*
Macro level	**Self-Consciousness**	*Self-Realization*
Mezzo level	**Mind**	*Self-Installation*
Meta level	**Spirit**	*Self-Monitoring*
Mini level	**Body**	*Self- Awareness*

<u>The Fractals of Spiritualized Beings</u>:

Living Intelligence + *Enlightened Self-Consciousness = A Whole Self!*

The desire to integrate oneself inside to be able to rationalize the reality outside must be nourished with the food for thought that is being transmitted to us from Above and that we, as part of the Universal Mind, are just learning to tune into digitally now. These grains of wisdom in their cognitive consonance soul-enhance us physically and emotionally.

Re-enforce your Spiritual Fractal's Unifying Force!

11. Don't Put Your Life in Recess; Be Life-Obsessed!

The inspirational, psychologically-charged rhyming boosters that you see at the bottom of each page are meant to help you better understand the refreshing minds and the insightful vision of *Edgar Cayce, Drunvalo Melchizedek, Dalai Lama, Dr. Frederick Bell, James Redfield, Deepak Chopra, Eckhart Tolle, Dr. Paul Pearsall, Dr. Wayne Dyer, Neale Donald Walsch, David Wilcock, Osho, Sadhguru* and many more other exceptional minds.

To be interesting, get interested!

We have a chance to be spiritually re-enforced by many inspiring ministers, like *Joel Osteen* and *T.G. Jakes,* as well as the most advanced soul-enriching scientists that I quote a lot in all my books. They inspired me to make my own modest contribution to the world's ever-growing **SELF-CONSCIOUSNESS** and its globally-responsible vision of life. If you want to belong to the world of the extra-ordinary people that I mention above, raising self-consciousness should become *an actionable, not just declarative thing* for you. Such focused and integrated approach to life attunes the mind and the heart, propels the spirit, and helps you attain the dream of your life. Unfortunately, the disconnection between the heart and the mind is always in the way. *One person is kind but does not have the mind! Another one is brainy but is heart-drained!*

So, accumulate the knowledge of the latest discoveries in different fields of science, generalize it., select what suits your beliefs and convictions, and actualize it, *working out your own science-verified system of Self-Actualization*, as the outcome of your holistically-processed work of putting the form and the content of your life together.

Form   +   Content

(Body+ Spirit+ Mind) +(Self-Consciousness + Universal Consciousness)

I keep working in this connection all my professional life. It's not an easy thing to change *the mentality, morality, and actuality* of my many intellectually-unmassaged, stubborn, and society indoctrinated students. Luckily, their minds and soul-refining do their work, and I enjoy the light of the hearts and minds that is reflected back to me inevitably in the outcome.

Nothing is Impossible if Self-Growth is Irreversible!

(End of Part One- Digital Re-formation)

Part Two

"Wisdom Outweighs Any Wealth."

(Sophocles)

Like sand on a beach, the brain bears the footprints of the mistakes that we make. Wash them off with a conscious storm of wisdom retort!

There is only one outcome for everyone under the Sun -

If you want to be above the ground,

Keep yourself happy and sound!

Choreograph Yourself in Every Cell to Self-Excel!

Give the World the Best You Have and Rationalize Your Life with Love!

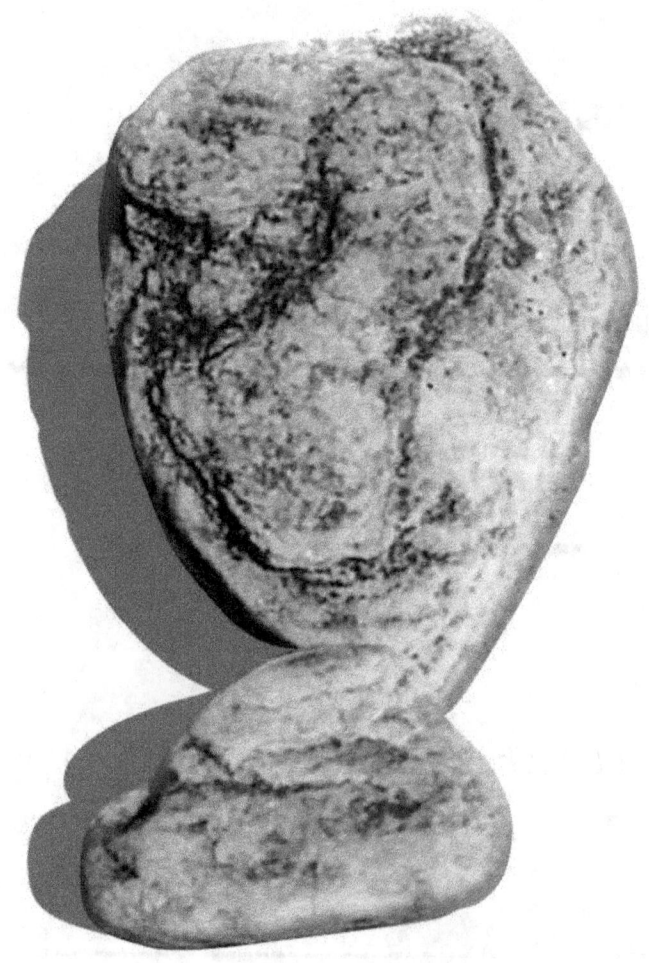

What am I here for?

Self-Awareness is in All, and All is Within You!

1. Soul-Perfection is the Way to Self-Resurrection!

To Unify
the Soul and Consciousness
as One is
the Goal of Everyone!

While you maybe disorganized, your brain isn't. You just must know how to help your brain maintain order and keep life-focused. Once you get rid of the mental clutter and the emotional mess, you'll become life-obsessed!

Don't Live on the Installment Plan,
Focus on the Self-Realization of Your Life Span!

2. Your Main Obligation is Your Self-Formation!

If you are heading to the Universal level of consciousness, you need to go beyond our physical addictive habits, the emotional turmoil, the mental chaos, and spiritual divisiveness. The Buddhist mantra in the Introduction as the main goal of this book, is helping you to finally come to your **INNER SELF-SALVATION,** or the universal level of the holistic paradigm of Self-Resurrection. At this stage of life, we integrate the wisdom, gained by us at the previous four levels: *physical, emotional, mental, and spiritual.*

Life-gaining is in knowledge obtaining and wise self-training!

It is extremely hard to squeeze self-discipline. into daily turmoil of life. I always hear from my students, *"I have no time for myself left."* **But if we do not time-oblige ourselves, we lose control over our cells.** They will have no leader, and therefore, will start *the process of physical, emotional, mental, and spiritual anarchy*. The cells are the citizens of the country that has your name and their happiness depends on the way the **PRESIDENT** or **YOU,** rules the country.

Your life-gaining is in self-taming!

If you qualify to ascend to the Universal level and get in touch with *the **Universal Field of Information**, the Source*, like the best of us do, your life will stop being senseless, reactive, impulsive and chaotic. It will get fully realized, and the ultimate objective of Self-Salvation will be accomplished, justifying the basic auto-suggestive rule of life - *to self-excel, you must program yourself* with the auto-induction that is the red line of all my books.:

I Can, I Want to, and I Will!

All the levels of the paradigm of Self-Resurrection are interconnected and are inter-penetrable, one, incorporating the other, like the Russian dolls, with ***the Mother Doll*** on top. So, instill order in your life in this fashion to thrive.

When you feel great, you modify your fate!

All the chunks of information here are backed up with the inspirational, rhyming boosters of psychological content to help you uplift your spirit and be strong in it.! The auto-inductive rule of happiness remains the same

Make your Heart Smart and the Mind Kind!

Be One of a Kind!

3. Self-Attune to Life without Any Strife!

The next basic rule is to learn *the Language of the interaction with life!* All the stages of self-resurrection are the stages of **SELF-INDENTIFICATION** and the constructive adjustment to life at every transformational stage with the help of self-education, balancing mediation, and Auto-Suggestive self-hypnosis.

Without consistent work at self-identification, there is no self-salvation!

Self-Awareness ⟹ **Self-Monitoring** ⟹ **Self-Installation**

Self-Realization ⟹ **Self-Salvation!**

Conscious interacting with life inwardly and outwardly is also teaching us to read the signs that the Universal Field of Consciousness is constantly sending to us *"in the form of numerous synchronicities".* (James Redfield) If you keep your **AUTO-ANTENNA** in the alert, *rationally+ emotionally -adjusted position*, you will inevitably get in touch with the inner musical Organ of your soul - .

Intuition is the HEART+ MIND Organ od the Soul that is whole!

This is the most important aspect of true self-awareness and life-awareness, and this is the way to **TRUE REALIZATION OF LIFE** that we all need to be aware of in the digital turmoil that has swept us and sucked us into its vortex.

Also, to see your life's flaws, be graceful with words!

Your thoughts are clothed in words, and the better and more positive words you chose to deal with your problems, the quicker the decision to solve them will come to you. *The channel of reception needs to be physically, emotionally, mentally and spiritually adjusted from the inception!* You need to recognize that any unconsciously-treated life situation plunges you into lower vibrations, that ruin the auto-antenna of the soul connection with the Universal Intelligence

Read into the life signs from the Above; that's your educational life stuff!

That's what is meant by the Hermetic principle of life that I comment on again and again in every book on self-creation. It is universal for all of us!

As it is Above, so it is below!

What is Essential is Invisible to the Eye."
(Antoine de Saint-Exupery)

4. Have a Clear-Cut Vision of the Self-Growth Provision!

(The Inspirational Booster)

Just wishing is refining,

But it's not life-defining!

    Not to let your dreams die

    You must learn to fly,

To fantasize, to realize,

To imagine and to visualize!

    Only with a clear-cut vision,

    Will you perform your journey with precision!

Don't Ever Whine, Shine!

No one provides congenial conditions for self-consciousness growth; it's the matter of your personal will's dose.

Form + Content

(Body + Spirit + Mind) + (Self-Consciousness + Universal Consciousness) = An Integrated and Life-Adjusted You!

The Main Auto-Induction:

I'm My Best Friend;
I'm My Beginning and My End!

5. We Are of the Fivefold Life Bind

We are of the fivefold life - bind:
The body, spirit, mind, soul, and the Universal Mind!

They are in a tight twine
With our evolutionary space and time!

Th soul resides in the future,
The body comes from the past,

The spirit and the mind
Are in the Now, thus!

The four dimensions of life:
Body, spirit, mind, and the soul

Intervene with Earth, Air, Water, and Fire.
That's what they define!
Which is the Dimension of Thine?

The answer is ready to be -
They are All in You and Me!

You Are the Owner of Your Life – So, Strive!

6. Our Consciousness Integration is the Way to Salvation!

Your life is determined by the level of your self-consciousness formation that is an integral process, as long as your life, and it needs aware attention paid to every stage of the holistic pyramid of your spiritualized self-actualization in life.

" Spirituality relates to the adulthood of our mind development." (J. Baines).

The mystery of consciousness is not unraveled yet, but our perception of the reality and conscious actions to change ourselves holistically make us the top of evolution at least in our universe. The highest aspect of an individual mind with its self-consciousness is Super-Consciousness, or the Universal Intelligence. Each of us has his / her own level of awareness of what Super-Consciousness means. In my understanding, the development of our intelligence cannot be adequately going on unless we get constantly aware of **the Universal Laws** and expand our cognition and perception of these laws in full integration with the physical, emotional, mental, spiritual, and universal levels of life.

The Grid of Our Consciousness Integration:

Super Level	*Consciousness of God!*	**Universal Dimension**
Macro Level	*Consciousness of the Universe*	**Spiritual Dimension**
Mezzo Level	*Consciousness of the World*	**Mental Dimension**
Meta level	*Consciousness of the Society*	**Emotional Dimension**
Micro Level	*Consciousness of a Man*	**Physical Dimension**

I think that the grid of consciousness development of both the society and the world that is presented above is being formed by an unprecedented socialization and globalization of our lives and minds now and our gradual consciousness ascending. We, in fact, develop *the holistic consciousness of* **INTER-DEPENDENCY** thanks to the digital revolution that is also integrally going.

Everything relates to everything. *"**Our Sun is the mind that guides the solar system; the Galactic mind guides the galaxy, and the Universal mind guides the Universe, the Source of the mind that guides all creation**."(David Icke)*

The process of upgrading of our **INTELLIGENCE + CONSCIOUSNESS**, viewed by me in five main philosophical levels holistically has helped me ***systematize the minds and intellectualize the hearts*** of hundreds of my students, propelling them to getting on the path of the never-dying aspiration to give the world the best they have. Order, knowledge, and inspiration do the magic work.

Solidify Your Soul with Discipline and Self-Control!

7. Spirituality is the Life Blood of the Universe!

We all need to raise the level of self-consciousness and integrate it with other levels of reality **TO HARMONIZE AND HUMANIZE** our souls. As a result of such integrity, we will see the world and ourselves in it in total connection with everything and everyone around us. All the levels are One inseparable unity.

The reality is multi-dimensional,

and every one of us is at a different level of his / her reflection of the reality.

At the Super Level of our consciousness development, we are attaining **Oneness with Life,** and the state of balance is ruling our essence, or, in other words, the time of our **INNER RENAISSANCE** finally arrives when we manage to integrate all the five levels of our being inside and outside. *Many intellectually-spiritualized people* have attained this unity. According to an amazing American visionary, **David Wilcock**, who, following the mind-boggling discovery of the fractal structure of nature by **Dr. Mandelbrot** writes, *"The entire Universe is a system of fractals, and the Universe is fractalized from a single point."*

I, in turn, have presented my vision of our spiritual fractals, above and in all previous books as the route of our **SPIRITUAL MAURATION**. We are thus forming our own fractals in the universal structure of life. *(See, Introduction, Chunk 4)* Can any machine ever be able to unify itself to this level?

Body+ Spirit+ Mind + Self-Consciousness + Universal Consciousness = a Refined Soul!

The fabric of space that, according to the latest developments in science, is *"the Quantum Energy Field of Information"* (*Dr. Richard P. Feynman*) is invisible, but it exists throughout the universe. The information is propagated though waves, called *quantum waves,* and it affects us at every level of life. The human brain is full of electrical activity, and every electron in our brains is a receiver.

"My brain is only a receiver."(*Nikola Tesla*)

We are supposed to take conscious care of our electrical circuit by performing our **SELF-CONSCIOUSNESS HYGIENE** at the *physical, emotional, mental, spiritual, and universal level*s in the conscious and consistent way. *(See Cycle One below*)

I Tune Myself to the Station God and Adjust My Thoughts to His Sacred Words!

8. Be Wise! Rationalize Your Self-Reforming Device!

We are unable to penetrate the secrets of the invisible core of life yet, but I believe that micro-part of the information that makes up *the Quantum Information Field* around us contains the electrons of the mental energy of the best of us, as well as the loving energy of our deceased loved ones.

The digitized brain is only in the self-expansion main!

The mental energy of the diseased people is in the extra-terrestrial aura of space, the aura that a great Russian scientist, *V.I. Vernadsky,* called the **NOOSPHERE - *the sphere of human thought.*** In the visionary theory of Vernadsky, the noosphere is the third in a succession of phases of development of the earth, after *the geosphere (inanimate matter)* and *the biosphere(biological life).* Vernadsky writes that just as the emergence of the fundamentally transformed geosphere, *the emergence of human cognition is fundamentally modifying the biosphere*, promoting **the LOVE CYBERSPACE** that we're probing now. The Super Mind is governing you in everything you do!

The human intellectual energy, or the eternal wisdom, is integrated into the ***Universal Consciousness Field*** and is emanated to us when we are perceptive enough to process this invaluable information. <u>The best is always abreast!</u> The latest developments in science accentuate the urgency of our *paying aware attention* to the **SOUL ECOLOGY** and stop going down the road of self-corrode. It means that you need *to synchronize your mind and the heart* in making decisions and solving whatever problem No inner renaissance is possible without such a connection because it also presupposes **the WHOLE BRAIN** *thinking. (See the book "Self-Taming!" for more).*

The problems of the disconnectedness between the brain and the mind, the mind and the heart come to the surface these days. It embraces the necessity to see any communication through the prism of a person's language habits and speech skills that are focused on his / her holistic self-re-formation. *The disconnectedness of both the right and the left hemispheres* in the brain knowledge-wise causes the problem because the brain is overwhelmed with the redundant information that a person gets digitally. The information should be sifted for its validity and gradually installed in the memory, so that *a person could operate his /her emotional mind better.*

Intellectualize Your heart and Emotionalize your Mind. Be One of a Kind!

9. Soul Renaissance is in Language-Speech Consonance!

The consonance of the brain and mind, as well as mind and the heart is hardly possible to be obtained without the inspirational value of <u>the AUTO-SUGGESTIVE LANGUAGE CODING</u> and a considerable reinforcement of the ***Psycholinguistic aspect of the Language Habits and Speech Skills connection.*** *(See the book "Language Intelligence or Universal English!".)*

The synchronization of the Brain + Mind function, or ***the whole brain thinking*** comes to the forefront next, and it is another urgent problem to be solved in our academic education. It is closely connected with the correct use of the language, especially English, called Globish now because there is no correct, insightful, digitally-enhanced, business-oriented thinking without the correct, less wordy, logical, and ***strategized use of the language,*** mostly English. Here is where the machine is surpassing us now, but our emotionally-enhanced intelligence is yet our main prerogative on the path of **THE TECHNOLOGICAL SELF-RESURRECTION.** The machines are accurate and precise in their self-expression. So, we absolutely need to t***ake care of the Language-Speech Awareness without thoughtless carelessness!***

The language information is often processed by us through the in-put and the out-put stages in an unconscious state. ***But the in-put and the out-put of the information should be in conscious connection.*** First, any problem needs to be well-constructed in the mind, then worded out. Slow thinking is the benefit here, not a deficiency, and the economy of speech is ***"the sister of talent."*** *(W. Shakespeare)*

Erosion of Language leads to the disruption of Speech!

The spiritualized intelligence that you are working on cannot be obtained without ***a tight language control. Educated language awareness is essential*** for your self-installation inwardly and outwardly. Language is the basis of our intelligence. and the most difficult one to monitor because it requires thorough shaping from berth. Attitude, grace, tact, looks, manners are generated in us by our parents and the environment. However, it's never too late to re-shape yourself, if need be. Self-controlled ***thinking-speaking skills*** can be taught and must be learned! Unfortunately, *numerous TV shows demonstrate de-magnetized yelling, cursing, aggressiveness, and reactive tongue-lashing.* Such language behavior becomes a habit that is very difficult to rid of. As a great Spanish linguist, *Fernando Lazaro Career*, most rightly noted,

"Language is the Skin of the Soul!"

10. Internalize Your Emotions and Externalize the Mind! Be One of a Kind!

<u>Watch your thoughts,</u>
For they become your words!
<u>Watch your words,</u>
For they become your actions!
<u>Watch your actions,</u>
For they become your habits!
<u>Watch your habits,</u>
For they become your character!
<u>Watch your character,</u>
For it becomes your destiny!

If "Happiness is an Hour Long,"
Be in a Hurry to start a Self-Reform!

11. Be Always Able to Say Without Any Dismay

(An Inspirational Booster)

Be always able to say

Without any dismay:

"I am unique in every

Stance

I was born, but only

Once!

There isn't, there wasn't,

And there won't ever be

Any one like

Me!

Thus, you will conquer the sky,

And you'll learn to soul - fly!

To Be Self-Inspiring and Self-Reflective,

Put the Mind + Heart unity into the Perspective!

P.S. Dear reader, please, note that it is impossible to present in detail every aspect I touch upon in all five books on Self-Actualization. As a college professor, I know that much information clogs the mind and the students' attention slags, lost in disconnected details. You can always enrich your outlook with the digital means. *Less is more! That's the Law!*

Never Stop to Celebrate a Happy Life's Ado of to Be, to See, to Give, and to Do!

(End of Part Two – Wise Awareness)

Part Three
The Incision to the Main Parts of the book)

The Five Cycles of Being

Learn the Art of Spiritualizing the Mind and the Heart!

"Follow the Dao;" *(Dr. Wayne Dyer)*

Live Consciously Here and Now!
Go Aboard the Extra-Terrestrial Fort!

(The Cross of Our Terrestrial Life Tree's There-Offs)

"There is No Lateness to the God's Call,"
So, Be in a Hurry to Self-Install! *(Vladimir Visotsky)*

Auto-Induction:
I Can Roam Any Terrain with God in My Vein!

1. Focus Your Seeing on Five Cycles of Being!

The conceptual structure and the philosophical background of every book on Self-Resurrection *(See Book Rationale)* together make up **the MANUEL OF LIFE** that I suggest educators prepare in five philosophical levels: *mini, meta, mezzo, macro, and super, or in **physical, emotional, mental, spiritual, and universal*** dimensions of the holistic self-creation.

In this final book, featuring the universal level of self-creation, I draw the parallel between these levels and the four levels that a great yogi mentor **His Holiness Maharishi Mahesh Yogi** has. According to the Yogi Master, *the Cycles of Being* consist of four stages: ***creation, maintenance, evolution, and dissolution.*** I add the third mental stage here as the intelligence enrichment, or *the Stage of Maturation.*

So, I see the **CYCLES OF BEING**, featured below as the main parts of this book, or as the *Universal Spiritual Route of* Self-Resurrection during the life time. In my understanding, the five stages that I have presented in all my previous books, are in parallel with the most insightful structure of Mahesh Yogi. It is our spiritual route *Beyond the Terrestrial,* one by one, and these are the names of the parts of this book.

Resurrect Yourself to the Universal Life Spell:

Stage Five ↑ **5. Dissolution** *(Super level – Universal dimension - **Self-Salvation***

Stage Four | **4. Evolution** *(Macro level - Spiritual dimension - **Self Realization***

Stage Three | **3. Maturation** *(Mezzo level - Mental dimension - **Self-Installation***

Stage Two | **2. Maintenance** *(Meta level- Emotional dimension– **Self-Monitoring***

Stage One | **1. Creation** *(Mini level - Physical dimension – **Self-Awareness***

As I have indicated above, the concepts of each part the book are illustrated by the *inspirational boosters* that are meant *to deliver the message of each part* in a poetic form and uplift your spirit to its final *Universal Dimension of Self-Resurrection* without any moralizing and with the sole intention to raise your life awareness and admiration with it.

Our hearts and minds get spiritually re-defined. Edgar Cayce, who I have the deepest reverence for, wrote, *"The whole field of life can be glorified by our taking care of Being at Each Stage."* Joel Osteen writes in one of his books,

"Success is Not an Elevator, It's a Set of Stairs!"

2. <u>Our Self-Salvation is in the Spiritual Maturation!</u>

I see a sure parallel of the **FIVE CYCLES OF BEING**, listed above, not only with the five stages of Self-Creation that I have presented as the route for Self-Resurrection in five books, but also *with a famous parable of Jesus Christ,* told to his disciples. I take the liberty to interpret it below as our five main stages in life. *<u>The wisdom of this parable is a great lesson for us to learn.</u>*

The Route of Self-Resurrection

The steps of the holistic self-growth and the books, featuring them:

5. Super - *Universal Level*	*Self-Salvation* -	Dissolution
4. Macro - *Spiritual Level*	*Self-Realization* –	Evolution
3. Mezzo - *Mental Level*	*Self-Installation* –	Maturation
2. Meta - *Emotional Level*	*Self-Monitoring* –	Maintenance
1. Mini - *Physical Level*	**Self-***Awareness* –	Creation

<u>The Parable for the Reader to Consider:</u>

1.The First Period of Life - <u>**Youth –Self-Awareness**</u> (Age 16-21- the age of romanticizing of life. - ***Creation)***

I am walking down the road.

I don't see the hole in it.

I fall into the hole.

-*"It's not my fault!"*

It takes a long time to get out of the hole.

2.The Second Period of Life – <u>**Self-Monitoring**</u> (Age 21-35 – *the* age of conformism and obtaining emotional self-control - *Maintenance)*

I am walking down the same road.

I see the hole, but I fall into it again.

- How come I'm in the same hole. Maybe, it's my fault."

It takes much less time to get out.

3. The Third Period of Life – <u>Self-Installation</u> (Age 35- 45 - the age of intellectual growth and the realistic perception of life. -*Maturation)*

I am walking down the same road.

I see the hole., however, I fall into it again.

"It's definitely my fault!"

I get out of the hole in no time.

----

4. The Fourth Period of Life – <u>Spiritual Evolution – Self-Realization</u> - (Age 45- 65 – the age of reason, life-awareness and spiritual maturity. – *Evolution)*

I am walking down the same road.

I see the hole.

I go around it!

----

5. The Fifth Period of Life – <u>Self-Salvation</u> (Age 65-85 + the age of wisdom and the universality of thinking – *Dissolution)*

I am walking down the same road.

I see the hole.

I take another road!

<u>*Drive though the time and space with knowledge and grace on your Life's Interface!*</u>

"Nothing so Needs Reforming as Our Habits."

(Mark Twain)

The Change May Be Slow, but It is, Sure, On the Go!

Our Past Lives

"The Fundamental difference between being alive and being dead is being conscious and unconscious." (Sadhguru)

You Must Beat the Self-Defeat!

3. Commit to Being Body+ Spirit + Mind Fit!

Accumulate wisdom in bits and store those bits in your memory that needs to be constantly monitored for the information that *you need to sift scrupulously* for its validity in your life transformation.

What you have uploaded into your memory programs your life!

Subjectively-processed *objective knowledge* restores the wiring between the heart and the mind and helps you to self-unwind! Every encounter with people also needs your *aware attention, or "executive attention" (Jeffrey Kluger)* to be applied because people often negatively program us if we let them do it.

In my life's course, I am my own boss!

Note it please that we also happen to meet people that we often remember not by their faces, but by the bits of valuable information that we pick from them and that boosts our creative thinking and eventually turns into grains of *personally-processed wisdom of life*. Be grateful to such people for your inner growth and enrich your **SPIRITUAL ARCHIVES** in the soul with such memories.

Don't compete and don't compare; Pick the best here and there!

The worst obstacle in life is fear!

The greatest mistake is a broken spirit!

The most dangerous person is a liar!

The most destroying feeling is envy!

The most beautiful action is forgiveness.

The best defense is a smile!

The unbeatable strength is faith!

Every good chess player knows that life is not just a black-white striped field. It's a chess board, and *your success on it depends on the moves you make* on it.

Don't Be Life-Moralizing; Be Life-Emphasizing!

4. Auto-Suggestive Psychology of Self-Ecology

To sum up the Incision to the main five life cycles of the book, let me remind you that there is a precious diamond inside you – **YOUR SOUL** This book is about ***observing Consciousness Hygiene in five Cycles of Being, presented above,*** heading to the Universal Dimension we all came from and are going to. They fully coincide with the five stages of the *Holistic Self-Actualization Paradigm.* Moving along this path, you are forming ***a spiritual fractal*** that is beautifying the life around into a more synthetic unity, making it more universal. ***Body + Spirit + Mind + Self-Consciousness + Super-Consciousness!***

The kaleidoscope of our refined souls is forming an incredibly-energized spiritual aura of balance, mutual respect, and tranquility that fill up the space around spiritually-intellectualized people that are forming ***the core of the fractal structure of the world.*** That's why such people always magnetize us with their personalities and self-processed wisdom. ***Going beyond the terrestrial*** means, therefore, going beyond our bad habitual ways of living automatically, materialistically, and pragmatically. We need to willfully suppress them consciously and continuously in the physical, emotional, mental, spiritual, and universal realms of life. As Mark Train said, *"Habit is habit and not to be flung out of the window by any man, but coaxed downstairs one step at a time."*

I suggest you apply the five **MAIN AUTO-SUGGESTIVE INDUCTIONS** below for your Self-Resurrection in five cycle of life holistically and consequentially. They correspond to the five levels of self-creation (*physical, emotional, mental, spiritual, universal* as ***creation, maintenance, maturation, evolution, and dissolution***, or in my vision as *Self-Awareness, Self-Monitoring, Self-Installation, Self-Realization, and Self-Salvation.*

The Basic Auto-Inductions for Self-Production:

1. I am My Best Friend; I am My Beginning and My End! - **CREATION**

2. I Make My Heart Smart and the Mind Kind! - **MAINTENANCE**

3. I Can, I Want to, and I Will! - **MATURATION**

4. I tune myself to the station God for His everlasting support! - **EVOLUTION**

5. I am You, and You are Me! We are in Unity! - **DISSOLUTION**

Consciously Monitor Your Life to Self-Derive!

(End of the Incision to the main parts- The Cycles of Being in the Universal Seeing)

Cycle One
(The Physical Dimension of Self-Resurrection)

Capture the Essence of Being!

Cycles of Being:

Mini Level – **Creation** *(Self- Awareness)*

Study the life stream, "surfing on its waves consciously."
(Ch. Kilham)

In the Long Run,
Everyone is Won by the Cycle of Evolution in its Initial and Final Solution!

Love Yourself the Way You Are!

(Am I an Ugly Duckling or a Swan?)

Even if You're an Ugly Duckling in your Inner Song, You Can Become a Beautiful Swan!

1. I Think What I Am, and I Am What I Think
If I Put Both Concepts in Sync!

I do not need
To justify myself;
I know who I am
In my every cell!

"*If you are unconscious, it's a crime against yourself!*"
(Sadhguru)

"***A Man doesn't go to Heaven, he goes to God!***"
(S. Lazarev)

Self-Induction:

I Do Not Whine; I Appreciate My Life Time!

2. To Soul-Refine, Envision the Holistic Paradigm!

To begin with, getting to the Universal Path of Self-Resurrection at the physical level, requires having *the vision of the holistic paradigm,* installed on the forefront of your mind from step one – *Self-Awareness,* inspiring you to do self-scanning and self-assessment daily, monthly, seasonally, and yearly in every of five levels holistically. Remember, *self-resurrection is not a step by step process.* It's a holistic growth at every level in the integral connection of one level with the previous one or the next ones. ***You must see yourself as Whole!***

During the winter self-evaluation session, we make up our new year provisions, reasoning out our mistakes and cleansing the soul with the white snow of a cooling meditation. **In spring**, we revitalize the spirit for a new coil of rising consciousness. **Summer** is the time of soul-maturation. **The Fall** is the time of accomplishments and self- realization.

Self-Resurrection Route:

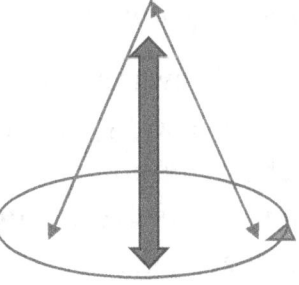

Universal Level	*Oneness*- Self-Salvation - **Dissolution**
Spiritual level	*Grace* - Self-Realization - **Evolution**
Mental level	*Mind* - Self-Installation – **Mental Enrichment**
Emotional level	*Spirit* – Self-Monitoring - **Maintenance**
Physical level	*Body* – Self-Awareness – **Creation**

Each coil is encircled within a vortex –*the spiral of the Universal Intelligence,* or the flow of information that guides the below levels higher with our growing *conscious life awareness* and a grateful perception of *the Now Moment* in unison with every season of life. David Icke writes very insightfully, *"The mind is the Sun that guides your solar system. The galactic mind guides the galaxy, and the universal mind guides the Universe."*

Move along with a grateful faith and inner grace!

Your mind, or your self-consciousness in action, is a small cell in this system, and it also guides *your own solar system* - your soul - *the* **HIGHER SELF** that you need to constantly control by enriching your intelligence and infusing your spirit with the suggestive word that nourishes both the *mind and the heart in sync,* inspiring you to go to the stars. The spirit energizes this unity and propels it to the stars, and, therefore, *it is in the center of the holistic paradigm:*

Body+ Spirit+ Mind + Self-Consciousness + Universal Consciousness

The Spirit is Our Perpetua Mobile!

3. Self-Awareness - What is It in Evidence?

So, ***self-awareness*** *is an integral process of self-knowing <u>at the physical, emotional, mental, spiritual, and universal levels.</u>* It is our life mission to know who you are and why you are here. In the holistic approach to life, self-awareness is the never-ending process of the **conscious, disciplined, controlled, and consistent self-growth and self-installation.** The main mind-set of all five books, is, actually, the title of the first one. "*I Am Free to Be the Best of Me!* It communicates the message of your exceptionality that you need to prove to yourself and the world.

I'm Not Life -Negligent; I'm Life-Intelligent!

Being life-intelligent means, you can answer the three main questions for yourself:

1) **Who Am I ?**   *(the main philosophical question)*

2) **Where did I come from?** *(the kind of person you were before)*

3) **Where am I going?** *(the kind of person you are going to be)*

Thank goodness, we are rapidly raising our self-awareness. We know how to operate our bodies better, how to retain more life energy, improve our health, and prolong the life span. We have an avalanche of information at every level of self-growth to answer these basic questions for ourselves, without mimicking anyone else's way of life. Let's quote G. W. F. Hegel again.

"Be the thing in itself!" That's your life's cell!

Think for yourself, develop your own thinking-critical skills, ***X-ray yourself, the people around you and the reasons for the events*** happening in your life. Analyzing the information in such a way, ***you get beyond your personal mental grid.*** That means that you take time to consciously select the information you need, and strategize your life according to ***your own plan of action***, guided by ***the objective Holistic Paradigm of Self-Actualization*** that I promote in all the books as:

a) Generalize and Internalize,

b) Select and Personalize,

c) Strategize and Actualize!

Synthesis – Analysis – Synthesis!

4. I Am a Homo Sapience!

(An Inspirational Booster)

I'm a homo sapience, yet I still belong
To the animal kingdom!

God commands, "Know Thyself!"
But I get back into my stereotyped shell!

I know so many things, yet I understand so little;
I am a phantom in the world of social litter!

I try to think for myself,
But I get lost in the common spell

Of the collective mind
Filled up with the totally blind!

I try to rise from my own ashes, as Phoenix,
But I fall back into the trap of human phonies!

"An eye for an eye, or a tooth for a tooth"
Remain in action, as the twisted truth!

To acquire the human quality
Do we need a 2000-year warranty?

Do we have to undergo another crucifixion
To stop taking Christ's story as a fiction?

                    True, many of us remain
                    In the anti-Christ domain!

The majority is still a victim
Of the collective dictum!

                    But there is a solution
                    For our human evolution

To stop being Homo Sapience
And become the Star People, hence!

We all need constant **SPIRITUAL RE-IDENTIFICATION** of self-formation that follows the fractal structure of nature, integrating our inner *ecology and psychology* in *the fractals of self-salvation:*

    Self-Awareness ➡ *Self-Monitoring* ➡ *Self-Installation*
        ➡ *Self-Realization* ➡ *Self-Salvation!*

Self-Synthesis ➡ *Self-Analysis* ➡ *Self-Synthesis!*
⬇   ⬇   ⬇
(self-awareness) ➡ *(self-monitoring +self-installation +self-realization)* ➡ *(self-salvation)*

Note, please, that such **self-harmonizing** can be accomplished with constant auto-suggestive **ACTABLE MEDITATION** that programs the cells, on the one hand, and cleanses the consciousness, on the other. **"Meditation is not an act; it's a quality!"** *(Sadhguru)*

Our Social Forte is in Harmonizing the World!

5. A Whole and Life-Adjusted You!

Thanks to the wonderful insight of *Daniel Goleman*, we know that we must work hard on our ***emotional intelligence***, our spirit, that is, in fact. our **MIND+ + SPIRIT +HEART** unity. Since we are more emotional, than rational beings at this point of our human evolution, we need ***to evolve our emotional set-up rationally -*** the physical form and the spiritual content in synch.

Form + Content

(Body+ Spirit+ Mind) +(Self-Consciousness + Universal Consciousness) = *A Whole and Life-Adjusted You!*

Unfortunately, too much energy is wasted at every level of our self-creation for impulsive actions because ***we are disconnected with the Universal intelligence, or the God's divine plan,*** and we often rely on our distorted vision of the reality. Therefore, our personal growth and dignity are essential in life. If you change the form of your knowledge, you are transforming your inner spiritual content because in the holistic paradigm of self-resurrection, ***the spiritual level goes after the mental one.*** Conscious, objective, individual, and aware vision is a must.

Objectively seeing the reality means having dignity and self-vanity!

Dignity means living at peace with yourself and the world. If your soul is full of love for life, for the **DIVINE WILL** in you, for your unique personal mission on Earth, no matter how small this mission seems to be to you, it's your duty to see and respect your exceptionality because you are an individual life. ***When you listen to the godly text in you***, report to God, and feel yourself as part of God, you are your own friend; ***you are your beginning and your end!***

Divinity, in turn, generates not just a blind religious obedience, but the emotional control, mental, and spiritual discipline, developing ***spiritualized intelligence*** in you naturally. ***It gets rooted only in the soul that is not governed by the society-indoctrinated values!*** Such a soul is channeled by the **HIGHER WISDOM of LIFE** that the best of us have. A great example of intellectualized spirituality is Sadhguru, a truly great role model to follow on this path.

Self-awareness is self-dignity, self-integrity, and self-magnetism!

Regrettably, we do not know ourselves because we mostly assess ourselves with the head, relying on someone's superficial assessment, not with ***the divine unity of the heart and the mind*** that protects the soul from being communized.

Being Self-Aware is Being Whole! That's Your Life's Goal!

6. Magnetize, Don't Demagnetize Your Soul-Device!

There is a lot of talk about the ways of obtaining success in life and becoming happier, but the venues to self-transformation are to be found *in our inner electro-magnetic formation*, or our *"inner engineering."(Sadhguru).*

"My body is electricity in action."(Nikola Tesla)

Personal magnetism must become our main ***"izm"*** that can illuminate and outshine nationalism, racism, sexism, or any other twist of the electro-magnetic field inside and outside of our bodies.

Every one of us is ***magnetically-charged*** with his / her thoughts, words, food and emotions, and the higher the charge is, the healthier a person is and the stronger is his / her determination to either construct life or let it get destructed. due to the lack of will-power, self- respect, and lack of personal magnetism, ***based on the mind + heart unity.***

An advanced informational biologist *Dr. Bruce Lipton*, the founder of ***informational medicine,"*** calls on us to obtain ***a new level of life-awareness about our biological and mental make-up*** to be able to shake off the old beliefs and re-program ourselves based on the new ones.

Dr. Lipton states that our digitally-educated idea of ourselves is a limited view that we are victims of a hereditary DNA. He believes that genes are not responsible for our personalities and lives, but ***"our programming of ourselves at the cellular level is."*** Such programming needs true, developed intelligence.

Life is not just a physical process, it's a digital phenomenon, too.

In the holistically-governed paradigm of self-growth, it is the holistic integration of the changes that a person undergoes in five main levels - ***physical, emotional, mental, spiritual, and universal.***

Another great scientist from Russia, ***the founder of space medicine***, an academician *Dr. Naumivakin,* writes that a cell is the primary energy-informational structure of life, and each cell, like a person, has its own functional capabilities. Dr. Naumivakin writes, *"we need to scan our bodies to feel how the cells work at a certain moment and see whether they work in consonance with the mind or in dissonance with it."*

Constant Self-Scanning is Soul-Refining!

7. Keep Your Soul Intact for Any Evil Act!

Our cells are the accumulators of energy, *the batteries that we need to charge with the spirit*. That's why I pace the spirit in the center of the holistic paradigm of self-resurrection - *the process of putting the form of life, its physical structure, with the content - your self-consciousness* in connection with the Universal Consciousness via your intuition and telepathic connection to life.

So, fix an AUTO-ANTENNA of the reception of the signals from the Universal Information Field and be inwardly up-beat!

Other than that, the balance of the form and content of life can be established not only if we manage to finally obtain the balance inside. It also needs to be installed *in our psychological environment -* the love life, our families, the job climate, business atmosphere, college environment, and the attitude that we display to the unknown people. The way people treat you, God does.

Every human contact is a responsibility!

The relationship between people must have the **FORM AND CONTENT** in sync, too! This is what my five books on Self-Creation are all about.

Form + Content

(Body+ Spirit+ Mind) + (Self-Consciousness + Universal Consciousness)

Life does not adjust to us, we adjust to life!

Remember *the main auto-induction for self-production* that I suggest you use at every level of Self-Resurrection to boost your spirit in any situation is:

I can, I want to, and I will!

(I'm becoming better and better with each coming day!)

This mind-set will also shield you against any negative moves and will fortify your will-power with the determination to resist the urges of immediate gratification of your whims.

To Be Life-Obsessed,

Make Life Cells-Programming Reassessed!

8. Your Immortal Soul Needs Conscious Control!

To Be a Butterfly in Spirit; Conquer the Four Elements of Life with it!

Do the Self-Talk

as the Auto-Suggestive Meditative Work!

"Eat less, walk more, laugh often, and love always!"

(The Tibetan wisdom)

To Be More Life-Fit,

Put on the Auto-Inductive Outfit!

Every Morning IS a Blessing!

Your Tree of Life must be Constantly ALIVE!

9. Learn to Thrive in the Four Elements of Life!

Learn to program yourself auto-suggestively in every cell for a new day and in sync with the **FOUR ELEMENTS OF LIFE** that govern it. I have first written about the absolute necessity of our connection with the four elements of life in the book "*Soul-Refining,*" featuring the emotional dimension of self-resurrection.

But the repetition is the mother of learning!

So, here we go:

Early morning – preparation procedure. When you wake up in the morning, don't be in a hurry to get up. Remember, your body is not a robot. It is alive, and you need to treat it as a living being consciously, giving it a chance to get back to the world of life. Harnessing the energy of the Sun on Earth, will give you access to an unlimited source of energy

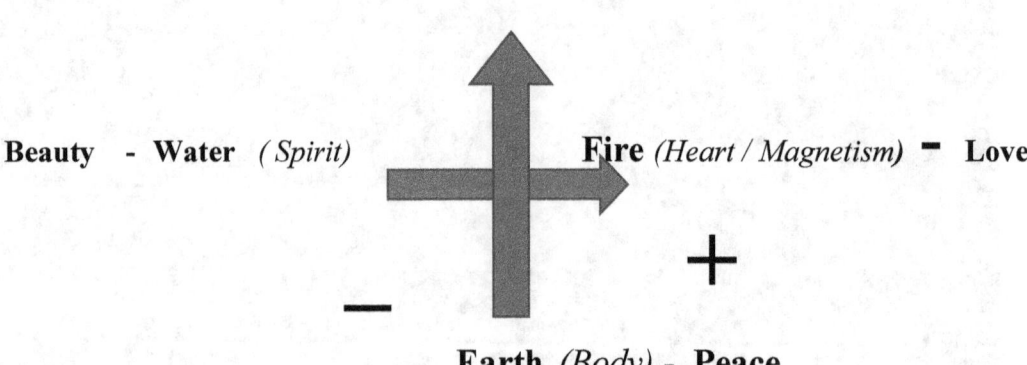

1. To begin with, inwardly **turn on the light in the body,** starting with the soles of your feet and finishing with picturing a bright light in the head, thus waking up every cell with the morning light that is washing you all from top to bottom. Feel the warms of life in you and express inner gratitude for it.

2. Move your eyes in the cross-like way.

   Life – Peace (*eyes up- down*) / **Beauty - Love** – (*eyes from the left to the right*)

Do the same in the opposite direction:

   Life – Peace (*eyes up- down*) / **Love- Beauty** (*eyes from the right to the left*)

Auto-Induction:

Life is Going on, and It's Beautiful in My Personal Form!

2. Next, to help the body experience getting awake, ***start rubbing the entire body with your palms,*** from the head to the neck, shoulders, the chest, the belly, the hips, the legs, and the feet. intensifying the pressure, going from the top to the bottom and feeling how all the cells come back to life. In the belly area, rotate your palms in a cycling fashion nine times clock-wise and counter clock-wise.

Now, ***stretch the entire body several times and slowly get up.***

----

1. <u>ELEMENT OF WATER</u>. In the morning, *b*efore getting into the shower, open the window in the bedroom and breathe in the fresh air of a new day. Then splash some cold water onto your face, clean your teeth in cold water, and drink a glass of water. Take a warm shower, ***inwardly reviewing your body from top to bottom with aware attention and care.*** Finish your showering with the water getting a little colder each morning until you feel quite comfortable to finish the shower with a splash of ice-cold water. It will refresh and energize the body and wake you up completely.

2. <u>THE ELEMENT OF AIR</u>. Your communication with air never ends, but try to breathe consciously, especially when you are outside. Start your working day with ***9 deep alternate breaths*** that will cleanse your left-right hemispheres and oxygenate the entire brain. To do that, close your right nostril with a thumb and breathe in through the left nostril.

Then, close the left nostril with your forefinger, opening the right nostril and breathe out through it. Alternate your breaths in this fashion. *Men should start breathing in through the right nostril.* **Breathe in** health, love, success; ***breathe out*** sickness, indifference, failure, etc. You can do the alternate breathing with any of the mind-sets in this book, breathing in the first part of it and breathing out the second one.

3. <u>THE ELEMENT OF FIRE</u>. a) The time of the power of fire comes at noon, and we need to fuel up our cells with the Sun rays. To warm up your cells, breathe in and out ***21 times.*** Doing that, look at the Sun, a lamp, a candle, or, on a rainy day, or just picture the Sun and your being warmed up by its energizing touch. Start doing ***alternative breathing of the sun rays*** through your nose. Breathe in the sun rays, inducting health, breathe out sickness, love vs. hatred, success vs. failure, piece vs. discord, etc. Burn them all out ***with the determination o**f **your inner flame formation.***

b) Looking at the Sun, *do some breathing of the Sun rays with your eyes*. Start breathing in through your left eye, closing the right one with a palm for a few second and breathe out through the right eye. Do the same breathing in the opposite direction. *The two electrical currents* (*in-out*) that you enact while such breathing, get electrified, filling up your body's electrical station with energy that determines your living during the day. Induct yourself with:

The Sun's rays guard all my ways!

If you feel uncomfortable meditating or doing anything that other people might be watching, disapproving, or sarcastic about, remember a very good Russian proverb:

"Dogs are barking, but the Caravan is walking!"

4. <u>THE ELEMENT OF EARTH</u> a) After 6 pm, when the Sun goes down, the Element of Earth comes to power. It brings us down to earth, calms us down, and prepares us for the night trip into the universal realm. Take a quick warm shower. Stepping out of the bathtub, shake off your body in the same fashion a dog does, coming out of water. All the problem out; let the earth process them into something better. Be thankful to the Earth for grounding them and freeing you of them. Induct yourself with the attitude of gratitude.

Thank you, dear God, for your Everlasting Support!

b*) Finally*, before going to bed, get totally undressed and lie down, *letting your body breathe in and out the cool of the coming night* in a very relaxed manner for a few minutes. Reflect on what good you have done during the day, thanking God for His support and asking for assistance with whatever comes / came your way.

Get under a warm blanket and *turn off the inner light, in the opposite direction, from the head to the feet,* gradually, consciously, and gratefully. Don't worry, any Gordian knot will be cut! Say inwardly assuredly:

<u>*No anger. no fear, no attitude, no joy smear!*</u>

Just say "Halt!" to the negative emotion Walt!

It'll get discharged with your awareness charge!

Sleep Tight and Accumulate Your Soul's Might!

10. Auto-Suggestive Meditation is Pivotal in Self-Formation

In all five books on the Auto-Suggestive Psychology of Self-Ecology, I describe different forms of active **Auto-Suggestive Meditation, or Self-Help Induction.** We can draw the parallel between the five levels of self-growth that are presented in all the books with five fingers on our hands and the necessity to meditate in four elements of nature. (See above)

Your will-power needs to be constantly activated because *it is the emotional gas of your spirit* that is the most important link between your body and the mind, or the mind and the heart that need to always be in synch in order to balance you.

The Cross is the Symbol of Unity the World Across!

Five fingers on our hands are amazingly linked to the five main action indications in every language: *the past, the present, the future, the process and the result of our life actions with the zero position of the soul's balance.*

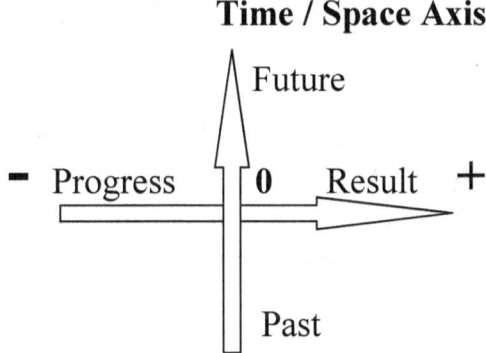

Breathing through the tips of the fingers, we establish the time-space linking, *training the body to live in the inseparable unity of the mind and the heart.*

I conduct the Active Auto-Suggestive Meditation with my students in the middle of the lecture, when I feel that their attention is slacking. They love it! Their aware attention gets charged, and they continue studying / perceiving my instructional in-put in a much more productive way. The auto-meditation also inspires them a lot. It's very simple but is very relaxing and invigorating.

*1) First **rub your hands vigorously and shake them off several times to cleanse the energy** that your hands have accumulated during the day.*

*Please, note first that when we put the central three fingers together and make the pinkie and the thumb go widespread to the sides, we, actually **get the cross** that is also the philosophic sign, representing the two vectors – **the vectors of time**) and **the vectors of space.***

By the way, the body of a standing man with his arms, stretched to the sides has the same structure

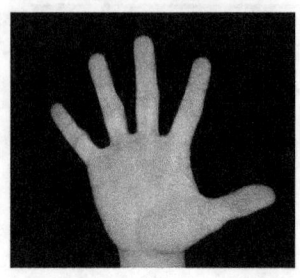

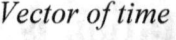

Vector of time

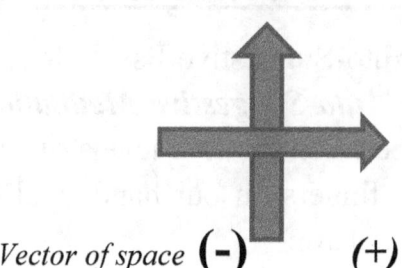

Vector of space **(-)**   **(+)**

*So, **by the Vector of Time**, we have - (the central finger- the **present**) ; the ring finger – **the-past** ; the index finger-**the future**)*

Going from **the pinkie** (*absence of result*) to the thumb(*the result finger*). *-from* **minus (-)** / *to plus* **(+),** we have **the Vector of Space**. No wonder we show the thumb in any language when things are great.

Enlighten Your Being with Better Feeing!

Do the inducting in the following way.

a) Imagine breathing through the pinkie on the left hand, with the eyes closed saying inwardly:

1)" *Life in going on* (*breathe in.*) Make a pause, ***focusing on the heart*** *-21-21-21. Finish the induction: - **and it's beautiful**"* (*breathe out through the pinkie of the right hand.*) *Channel the air stream up the left arm, the shoulder, making the pause at the heart and channeling the breath down the right shoulder and the arm to the tip of the pinkie on the right hand.*

2) *"**I forgive myself** (Breathe in through the ring finger on the right hand) – **Pause at the heart! - all my past mistakes**". (breathe out though the ring finger on the right hand)*

3) *"**I live** (Breathe in through the central finger) – **Pause** / focus on the heart -21-21-21- **consciously and joyfully**.(Breathe out though the central finger on the right hand.)*

4) *"**I will do** (breathe in though the index finger) – **Pause** -   **whatever I plan to**" (breathe out through the index finger of the right hand)*

5) *"**I have already** (breathe in through the thumb of the left hand) – **Pause – done a lot!**" (breathe out through the thumb of the right hand.) Envision what you have done lately.*

 After you have practiced such breathing a couple of times, you will literally feel a slight breeze ***at the tips of your fingers*** when you breathe out.

----

b) *Next,* breathe in and out in the opposite direction, starting with the thumb of the right hand and breathing out though the thumb of the left hand. Continue breathing in the same fashion through all the fingers. *Don't forget to channel the* *energy with the help of aware attention up the arm, through the chest, down the other arm, out through the corresponding finger. Don't forget to make a loving pause at the heart.*

The auto-inductions should be a bit changed, and you should finish with the same induction that you started the inducting with:

Life is going on and it's beautiful!

Breathe in and out slowly and mindfully.

1) *The thumb –* **"*I have already*** *(breathe in),* **Pause at the heart-** ***accomplished a lot.*** *" (breathe out). Envision your latest accomplishments*

2) *The index finger -* "***I will do*** *(breathe in) –* **Pause –** ***even more.*** *" (breathe (out) Envision what you want to do)*

3) *The central finger –* "***Because I live*** *(breathe in)-* **Pause -** ***consciously and joyfully***". *(breathe out)*

4) *The ring finger –* "***Because I forgave myself*** *(breathe in)* **- Pause -** ***all my past mistakes.***"*(breathe out)*

5) *The pinkie – "* ***My life is going on*** *(breathe in)-* **Pause –** ***and it is beautiful!***" *(breathe (out)*

Concluding the auto-inducting, open your eyes and say authoritatively inwardly, or better out loud:

In my life quest, I am the best!

There wasn't, there isn't, there won't ever be

Anyone like me! or

<u>***I am my Best Friend; I am my Beginning and my End!***</u>

"Don't be afraid to open the door to do things you've never done before."

"The Best is Yet to Come!" *(Carolyn Leigh)*

11. Be a Cosmic Strategist!

(An Inspirational Booster)

You are a good strategist in mind, but a slow tactician in action;
You are in constant mind fraction!
You can analyze and generalize, visualize and prioritize,
But you are not overly wise!
You often fall back
On your self-pity track
Your emotionally-charged inner car
Is not mind-efficient poka! (Russian "not yet)
You lack reasoning, tenacity, and perseverance
You need self-love without indifference!
You are often sick with your own face;
You are permanently on your case!
If you do not fuss,
Your life will collapse!
You need to practice the Law of Attraction;
You must fix your emotional fraction!
The law will change the polarity
Of your self-pity vanity!
You'll get re-harmonized
And become wise!
There is no time for delay,
Nor there's space for self- dismay!

The Law of Gravity at work

Springs up the spiral of your talk.

It'll manifest

What you've professed!

For "what you think about,

You bring about!"

It'll turn the fantasy into a fact

Without any doubtful pact!

So, let's put a wish up there

And try to always be ware

That attitude of gratitude

Needs to be your new aptitude!

Think of luck, love, money, and success

And visualize them to an excess

When you visualize,

You strategize and materialize

Not the what, but the How,

And you'd better do it Now!

The Ocean of Consciousness out there

Oversees you to be more aware!

To Have No Inner Fraction,

Become a Cosmic Strategist in Mind and an Honest Tactician in Action!

12. Stop Being a Dope!

(An Inspirational Booster)

Stop being a dope;

　Expand your mental scope!

　　　　　Raise your human height

　　　　　With the spiritual might!

――――――――――――――

Stop problem mounting

　And doubt sprouting,

　　　　　　Action fearing,

　　　　　　And love smearing!

Stop lying to yourself and others

In hazy make-believe devours!

　　　　　　Also, stop obsessing,

　　　　　　And emotionally recessing,

　Prejudging and cheating,

Double-dating and date-omitting!

　　　　　　Stop talking too emphatically

　　　　　　And praying automatically!

Stop overeating and dieting,

Being lazy and rioting,

　　　　　　Yelling, evil-defining,

　　　　　　And fist-refining!

　Stop drugging and alcohol consuming,

Abusing and fight-booming!

Stop self-justifying, blaming and whining,
And always police–undermining!
Stop mind-revolutionizing,
But not actualizing!
Stop junk-installing and texting,
Nonsense uploading and reflexing,
Utilizing Internet pornography
And destroying marriage monogamy!

If this profile
Is in your style,
Change it and break free
To save the remnants of your soul's glee!
Thus, you'll stop staying in the snares of sin,
And you'll make all the vices obscene!

But if you don't follow these precautions
And keep giving up to set-backs and evil abortions,
Vices will bring you to the point of no return,
And devil will blow his final horn!
Remember, conformity and deformity
Are in a mirror-like unity!
Only a pure mind and a kind heart
Will fortify your over-reactive gut!
They'll strengthen your immunity

To a poisonous life deformity!

Your form and content will come in synch,

And your soul will get God's approving wink!

DON'T GET OUT OF your FORM,

Don't let it be twisted by an EVIL DEFORM!

Nothing Beats Where an Honest Soul Fits!

Get in the habit of watching what the state of your self-consciousness is and what is necessary to do for its ecology. Do the **SELF-SCANNING** every night to feel how the body feels and whether it is in consonance or dissonance with your spirit and the mind. Your *conscience will be the tester* of the health of your soul.

<u>Form + Content</u>
<u>(Body+ Spirit+ Mind) + (Self-Consciousness + Universal Consciousness) = *a Balanced You!*</u>

Learn to meditate on the unity of all five ingredients of your soul. Inner objective X-raying yourself and boosting your energy through auto-suggestively-governed breathing will help you balance. (*See* **the Auto-Suggestive Meditation** *in the book "Living Intelligence or the Art of Becoming!*

So, Don't Put a Long Face on Your Soul's Interface!

Don't Perform the Soul's Striptease, and

Don't Freeze Your Dreams!

"Seek and You Will Find,"

If you Unite the Body, the Heart, the Spirit, and the Mind!

Every Step May Be Stability-Bereft!

But Life is Going on,
And It's Worth Your Having Been Born!

13. Don't Just Survive; Be in Love with Life!

Any Creation is Life Elation!

"Joy-ology" is my Psychology!
(Dr. Paul Pearsall)

Auto-Induction:

I am happy no matter what;

Happiness in my Full -Time Job!

Consciously Infuse Your Self- Revitalization Fuse!

14. Be Also a Sage - Manage Your Age!

(An Inspirational Booster)

Being young

Is a part of the Universal Plan!

   So, every new day's spin,

   I command to my life's gene:

"I am 27 and not a day more!

I am as young as ever before!

   I am dynamic as ever;

   I am sluggish never!

I was, I am, and I will be young

Forever!"

   I defy your age

   With a graceful rage!

I face it with a charm

Of an irresistible man / femme!

   Thus, I live in the trinity

   Of God, Love and Infinity!

"It's Worth Every Treasure on Earth to Be Young at Heart!"

(With Frank Sinatra's song stay soul-warm and live long !)

15. I Have Set the Limit!

To accomplish all that I can,

I have set the limit for my life's span!

        I want to be young in my stem

        And live till a hundred and ten!

To be beautiful and young

Is a natural fun!

        But, to be wise and attractive when you are old

        Requires a very special mold!

You need to train your mind

To be selective and kind!

        You must make your body

        Walk straight and embody

Grace, patience, tolerance, and calm

To get people magnetized and love-stung

        With your wisdom and spiritual potency

        That you leave behind as your eternal legacy!

Thus, with a strong spirit's stem,

You'll live to a hundred and ten!

"Wisdom comes with age, but sometimes age comes alone."

(Ancient wisdom)

Staying Young and Not Age-Obsessed,

Gets Excessive Happiness Mind-Processed!

16. Observe the Fractal Unanimity of Your Soul's Infinity!

Concluding to review of the first cycle of life in the physical dimension, let me draw your attention to the absolute necessity to shed *the burden of judgments and self-justification* to **CLEAN YOUR SOUL'S OASIS.** You need to observe your **self**-consciousness hygiene every day, lying in bed at night, after your final prayer. A self-monitored soul hygiene requires *aware attention* Such procedure will teach you to *magnetize your inner self* and develop strong **PERSONAL MAGNETIZM** that we call charisma. Mind you, drugging, drinking, quick-fix relationships, cheating, gossiping, fighting, etc. *demagnetize the soul.* Healthy personal magnetism is the core of optimism and stamina and it is impossible without holistic self-development and constant S*elf X-raying* to preserve the **FRACTAL UNANIMITY** of the soul. Getting to scan thyself, you are getting to know the God's spiritual spell!

Increase the psycho-tonic energy - the energy of your spirit!

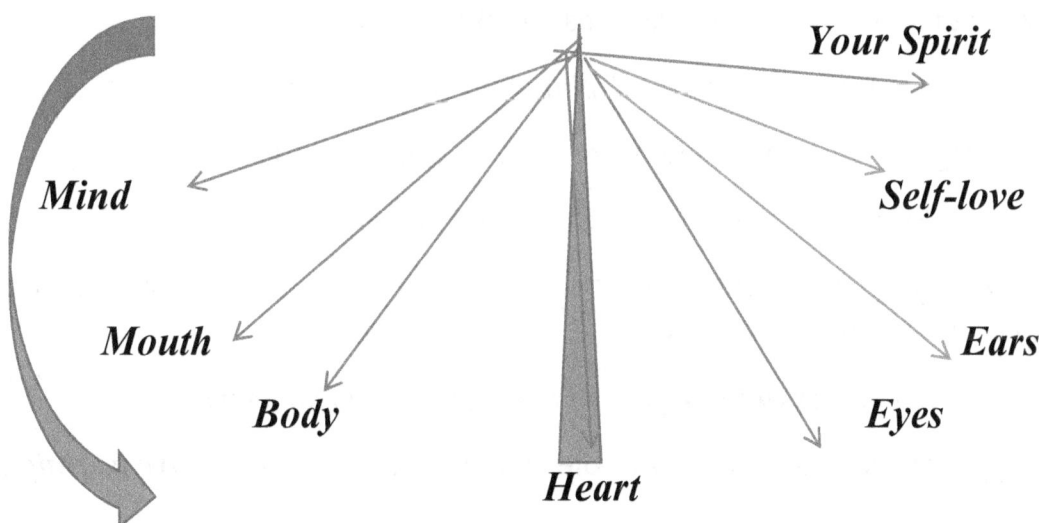

Your life will have a different quality depending on the level of your life awareness – your personal magnetism - *the unity of your heart, the spirit, and the mind,* essential for your self- consciousness.

You will gradually develop a very good habit of meditating *to review your insides for their spiritual hygiene,* in the same way as you take care of your exterior. It's the best soul-refining habit. So, every day, as time allows, shake off the old, dry leaves from your *"Tree of Life"*, and let it grow new, spring leaves - strong, fresh, and green.

Auto- Induction: by Neale Donald Walsh

"Be Conscious! "Consciousness Mobilizes!"

17. Have Enough Dignity to Protect Your Hygienic Unity!

1. **_Protect your mind_**! Make intelligence the main motor of your life! Store some auto-suggestive injections to be always brain sharp. Don't cast negative spells on your sells!

Don't assume negative thoughts perfume!

2. **_Protect your body_**! Never harm or pollute your body! Do not destroy its inner rhythm, its harmonious music of health and a strong spirit.

Clean it and nourish it to be life-fit!

3. **_Protect your mouth!_** Mean what you say and say what you mean! Don't hide your exceptionality in banality.

Foul words are language sanity warts!

4. **_Protect your heart!_** Make your mind kind and your heart smart! Deny yourself the luxury to react, be on a control response track!

Learn the Art of Seeing with your Heart!

5. **_Protect your eyes_**. Clean your sight from envy, lust, and ugliness.

Eyes are the mirrors of the soul and self-console!

6. **_Protect your ears!_** Don't let gossip, foul language, bad stories, or any other life cacophony destroy your inner harmony.

"All comes to the sound of life." (Sacred Geometry)

7. **_Protect your spirit!_** Don't be a low pole, a mope, or a sad sack! **Have a straight back!**

8. **_Protect your self-mage!_** Love yourself first to be able to love others!

9. **_Avoid a comparison trap!_** Be in a unique yourself wrap!

10. **_Being holistically-conscious_** means cultivating love, sent from the Above!

"Discipline your thoughts, words, and deeds!

(Proverb 19,27)

"Vitality comes from Your Spirit and the Soul."

So, Be Overly Whole! *(Jerry Seinfeld)*

18. Develop Alert Life Awareness!

Finally, on the path of your physical self-transformation, start paying *aware attention to the meaningful coincidences and different signs in life* with a new nurturing substance – **ALERT LIFE AWARENESS!**

Reflecting on life rationally and consistently at each of the five stages through the prism of ten most vital intelligences that I consistently remind you of in every book *(See "Living Intelligence or the Art of Becoming!")*, we can and must enrich our souls consciously and expand our kindness exponentially. <u>*Aware attention to self-development in each of the five cycles of life defines conscious evaluation of the quality of your life.*</u> It toughens up your willpower and disciplines your response to the life's troubles that are supposed to be there according to the cosmic *Law of Vibration*, anyway.

<u>**Induct yourself with Life-Awareness of Fairness!**</u>

I am fearless and hate-less;

I am ageless and time-less!

I am less than I can profess,

But I am more than I was before!

My transformation is slow,

But it is meant to go

Far beyond the vision

Of my every day's provision!

So, my New Year resolutions

Are full of wonderful solutions

To build up my New Life's Fort

And go forward!

"Be Aware of This Moment; It's Your Life!"

<u>*(End the Physical Cycle of Self-Inducting)*</u>

Cycle Two
(The Emotional Dimension of Self-Resurrection - a)

Dissonance

Cycles of Being:

Meta Level – **Maintenance** *(Self-Monitoring)*

"Life is too long and too short.
Too long for the weariness of "I"; too short for the work to be done." (Mark Twain)

Inspiration or Desperation – That's the life's Equation!

Life without Emotional Negligence is the Main Prerogative of the Emotional Intelligence!

Love of a Lower Vibration is even in Rock-Formation!

Emotional Stability is in Love's Infinity!

1. The Steering Wheel is in Your Spirit Still!

Be Emotionally-Smart; Learn the Art of Spiritualizing Your Mind and the Heart!

Power is in the Peace of the Inner Bliss!
(The Tibetan Philosophy)

Become an Artist of Your Own Framing!

2. "We Develop Only When We Train!" *(Aristotle).*

I have indicated in every book that your developing along the holistic paradigm of self-creation is not a step by step action. *It's an integral process* that is inseparable from any of the levels that you need to keep in mind and channel yourself by.

The aware attention has to be consistently paid to performing of your *spirit's hygiene.* You need to generate constructive energy and learn to **CHARGE YOUR SPIRIT** from the Universe, the Mother Nature, the Sun, the Moon, the four elements of nature, the food you eat, and the air you breathe. Most vital is your establishing *the connection with your cells* - your inner population.

Change yourself, working with your cells!

It means that you need *to scan yourself regularly* with the aware attention paid to the state of your inner organism and tune it like a musical instrument to health, vitality, contentment for being alive and gratitude to the Universal Intelligence that we call God for the chance of living and enjoying life in all its fluctuations.

I have developed the habit of *listening to the classical music to enhance my brain and body cells* and to adjust my mood should it happen to sag. I listen to *Mozart* to uplift my spirit, to *Beethoven* or *Shonen* to boost my decision for action, to *Vivaldi* for a romantic set-up, relaxation or meditation, to *Bach* to get inwardly connected to God before or during my *active Auto-Suggestive Meditation.* I raised my kids with the classical music in the background of their playing games to develop their brains and to expand their emotional make-up.

Pay aware attention to your inner world without any retention!

Check out *the Auto-Suggestive Meditation* in the previous books, especially the books "Soul-Refining" and Self-Taming. see what resonates with your personally and work out your ownmethods for boosting your spirit.:

The Holistic Self-Actualization Pyramid / Books, featuring these stages:

5. *Universal level*	*Self-Salvation*	" Beyond the Terrestrial!"
4. *Spiritual level*	*Self-Realization*	" *Self-Taming!*"
3. *Mental level*	*Self-Installation*	" *Living Intelligence of the Art of Becoming!*
2. *Emotional level*	*Self-Monitoring*	" *Soul-Refining!*'
1. *Physical level*	*Self-Awareness*	" *I Am Free to Be the Best of Me!*"

Be Emotionally-Wise!

Don't Immobilize the Spirit's Device!

3. Constant Dissonance Destroys Us in Mass!

(An Inspirational Booster)

We suffer from a constant dissonance
That's the absence of the heart and mind's joint dance!

Dissonance produces tension and instability,
And it results in a conflict and a disability!

But our terrestrial dissonance
Can be turned into an extra-terrestrial consonance

If we help its agreeable sounding
Appease our minds and hearts' pounding!

The cosmic consonance will add harmony and balance
And it'll help us emotionally bounce

The urge to hit the other's cheek
If yours was beaten with a stick!

Consonance has a harmonious core,
It preaches to us with, "Less is more!"

It also shifts education to a new paradigm pole
To see oneself and life as a whole!

So, let's turn our inner dissonance
Into the eternal global consonance

And allow our terrestrial life continuation
Have a sense of balance, peace, and elation!

Only being truly intelligent, calm, and glad
Can we accomplish all that!

"We live in a topsy-turvy world. Everyone destroys himself, or someone and something. Doctors destroy health. Lawyers destroy justice. Universities destroy knowledge. Governments destroy freedom. Religion destroys spirituality." *(David Icke)*

Let's practice what we preach without any spirit's breach!

"When you choose the behavior, your choose the consequences" *(Carl Jung)*

Self-Induction:

You Radiate What Your Emotions Emanate!

4. To Be Inspired, Be Self-Inspiring!

We are living in a radically transformed and transforming world and adjusting to it is becoming tougher and tougher with each day. Life is continuously casting problems and disappointments, *testing our emotional stability and psychological hardiness*. The mind-sets that are used at the bottom of each page and the inspirational, psychologically backed-up boosters are meant to serve as *the food for your spirit* that is the link between the heart and the mind - the basis for your **ASCENDING SELF-CONSCIOUSNESS** and inner stability.

Body+ Spirit+ Mind + Self-Consciousness Universal Consciousness
A New, Inwardly-Integrated You!

In the struggle for self-installation in life, *we all make the choice* to either go with the flow of the common sense life and be cast away by the brutal competition for a place under the Sun or *go against the current* and be a winner in this competition between evil and goodness, self-control, and self-neglect, hate and love, life and death. Having outlined in the previous four books the conceptual structure of my vision of a person's holistic route of Self-Resurrection I realize that I have nothing to add to what has already been written, but one fundamental thought:

Heaven in not somewhere above the Earth. It's on the Earth!

We cannot go beyond the impenetrable **UNIVERSAL LEVEL** of life unless *we start appreciating life itself,* accepting the reality the way it is!

"Life is tough! - Compared to what?" (Daile Carnegie)

We cannot find happiness and contentment, unless we start seeking the ways of uniting with all life in an overwhelming desire to express our gratitude for the gift of life that is granted to us from the Above.

There is no other life beyond being alive!

Be grateful to yourself, too, because despite the troubles and tribulations of life that you, for sure, have experienced so far, *you keep being life-fit and life-inspired.* Every one of us has his / her share of life's twists and turns.

They should not make us bitter, they must make us better!

Self-Induction:

I Celebrate My New Self without Any Negative Spell!

2. "We Develop Only When We Train!" *(Aristotle).*

I have indicated in every book that your developing along the holistic paradigm of self-creation is not a step by step action. *It's an integral process* that is inseparable from any of the levels that you need to keep in mind and channel yourself by.

The aware attention has to be consistently paid to performing of your *spirit's hygiene.* You need to generate constructive energy and learn to **CHARGE YOUR SPIRIT** from the Universe, the Mother Nature, the Sun, the Moon, the four elements of nature, the food you eat, and the air you breathe. Most vital is your establishing *the connection with your cells* - your inner population.

Change yourself, working with your cells!

It means that you need *to scan yourself regularly* with the aware attention paid to the state of your inner organism and tune it like a musical instrument to health, vitality, contentment for being alive and gratitude to the Universal Intelligence that we call God for the chance of living and enjoying life in all its fluctuations.

I have developed the habit of *listening to the classical music to enhance my brain and body cells* and to adjust my mood should it happen to sag. I listen to *Mozart* to uplift my spirit, to *Beethoven* **or Shonen** to boost my decision for action, to *Vivaldi* for a romantic set-up, relaxation or meditation, to *Bach* to get inwardly connected to God before or during my *active Auto-Suggestive Meditation.* I raised my kids with the classical music in the background of their playing games to develop their brains and to expand their emotional make-up.

Pay aware attention to your inner world without any retention!

Check out *the Auto-Suggestive Meditation* in the previous books, especially the books "Soul-Refining" and Self-Taming. see what resonates with your personally and work out your ownmethods for boosting your spirit.:

The Holistic Self-Actualization Pyramid / Books, featuring these stages:

5. Universal level	*Self-Salvation*	" Beyond the Terrestrial!"
4. Spiritual level	*Self-Realization*	" Self-Taming!"
3. Mental level	*Self-Installation*	" Living Intelligence of the Art of Becoming!*
2. Emotional level	*Self-Monitoring*	" Soul-Refining!'
1. Physical level	*Self-Awareness*	" I Am Free to Be the Best of Me!"

Be Emotionally-Wise!

Don't Immobilize the Spirit's Device!

3. Constant Dissonance Destroys Us in Mass!

(An Inspirational Booster)

We suffer from a constant dissonance
That's the absence of the heart and mind's joint dance!

Dissonance produces tension and instability,
And it results in a conflict and a disability!

But our terrestrial dissonance
Can be turned into an extra-terrestrial consonance

If we help its agreeable sounding
Appease our minds and hearts' pounding!

The cosmic consonance will add harmony and balance
And it'll help us emotionally bounce

The urge to hit the other's cheek
If yours was beaten with a stick!

Consonance has a harmonious core,
It preaches to us with, "Less is more!"

It also shifts education to a new paradigm pole
To see oneself and life as a whole!

So, let's turn our inner dissonance
Into the eternal global consonance

And allow our terrestrial life continuation
Have a sense of balance, peace, and elation!

Only being truly intelligent, calm, and glad
Can we accomplish all that!

"We live in a topsy-turvy world. Everyone destroys himself, or someone and something. Doctors destroy health. Lawyers destroy justice. Universities destroy knowledge. Governments destroy freedom. Religion destroys spirituality." *(David Icke)*

Let's practice what we preach without any spirit's breach!

"When you choose the behavior, your choose the consequences" *(Carl Jung)*

Self-Induction:
You Radiate What Your Emotions Emanate!

4. To Be Inspired, Be Self-Inspiring!

We are living in a radically transformed and transforming world and adjusting to it is becoming tougher and tougher with each day. Life is continuously casting problems and disappointments, *testing our emotional stability and psychological hardiness*. The mind-sets that are used at the bottom of each page and the inspirational, psychologically backed-up boosters are meant to serve as *the food for your spirit* that is the link between the heart and the mind - the basis for your **ASCENDING SELF-CONSCIOUSNESS** and inner stability.

Body+ Spirit+ Mind + Self-Consciousness Universal Consciousness
A New, Inwardly-Integrated You!

In the struggle for self-installation in life, *we all make the choice* to either go with the flow of the common sense life and be cast away by the brutal competition for a place under the Sun or *go against the current* and be a winner in this competition between evil and goodness, self-control, and self-neglect, hate and love, life and death. Having outlined in the previous four books the conceptual structure of my vision of a person's holistic route of Self-Resurrection I realize that I have nothing to add to what has already been written, but one fundamental thought:

Heaven in not somewhere above the Earth. It's on the Earth!

We cannot go beyond the impenetrable **UNIVERSAL LEVEL** of life unless *we start appreciating life itself,* accepting the reality the way it is!

"Life is tough! - Compared to what?"(*Daile Carnegie*)

We cannot find happiness and contentment, unless we start seeking the ways of uniting with all life in an overwhelming desire to express our gratitude for the gift of life that is granted to us from the Above.

There is no other life beyond being alive!

Be grateful to yourself, too, because despite the troubles and tribulations of life that you, for sure, have experienced so far, *you keep being life-fit and life-inspired.* Every one of us has his / her share of life's twists and turns.

They should not make us bitter, they must make us better!

Self-Induction:

I Celebrate My New Self without Any Negative Spell!

5. Don't Be Stiff; Get Rid of the Negative "If!"

(An Inspirational Booster)

If anything, negative ever occurs.

Immediately change your electro-magnetic course!

Switch your Amygdala

To the front lobes' mental gala!

Celebrate every minute of your stay

In the world of no dismay!

Say "Hurray!" to every day,

Stretch your hand to everyone on this land!

Say, "Hello!" to every living thing

Up and below!

Direct your mind

To a positively-conscious re-wind!

Learn to operate the Amygdala handle

In unity with your mental bundle!

Become a Star Man

With the mentality of the One!

Stressing is losing energy and the unity with the Self and God!

Your Goal is to Master

the Inner Devils that Lead to a Disaster!

6. To Be More Life-Fit, Snap Out of It!

Bad circumstances in life have one cure - ***tolerance, endurance, and honest analysis of the reasons*** of the life complications that you must face. They are always generated by our ignorance, impulsivity, attitude, or sheer stupidity.

Unconscious life dealings result in life cells killings!

Last year, I got the unbearable news from Ukraine. My son was killed there by the people who grudged the fact that he was pro-Russian. He was raised in a very friendly country of no discrimination, but his views were alien for those who has poisoned the minds of the people with nationalism and separatism.

The unprecedented hate that had swept all Ukraine and caused this loss for me resulted in the urgent necessity to help myself get over the unbearable pain that will stay with me my entire life. I owe my re-berth to his wife, left with a newly born son and the rest of the family that is living now in fear and utter uncertainty of the future.

This life test made me think about writing the fifth book in the series of book on personality formation, ***"Beyond the Terrestrial,"*** devoting it to my son and completing the holistic paradigm of self-creation that I had been working on against all odds. The question about what happens to us beyond the terrestrial boundaries has been probed by the people for centuries, but I am not going to explore ***what happens to us then, in the un-answerable when.***

I want us to wake up to the value of life holistically, consciously and inspirationally now. The auto-inductive work, or self-hypnosis helps us fortify our spirit and accomplish what you want and whenever we want it. We do self-hypnosis or self-talk nonstop, but, most of the time, the inner chatter box is beyond our managing, and ***"we let our thinking go loose and lead us astray."*** *(Eckhart Tolle)*

CONSCIOUS SELF-HYPNOSIS is not letting your mind switch into a regular chatter–box mode. It keeps the mind focused on ***"the Volitional I"*** perfection and helps you become ***stronger-spirited*** at its formation. Emotionally and mentally integrated **SELF-PERSUASION** is a special personal gain or the opportunity to avoid trouble and achieve your goal through the rational behavior, strengthened by the never sagging spirit. Induct yourself with: ***Life is tough, but I'm tougher!***

Consciousness Hygiene is Our Life's Magic Gene!

7. Don't Be Self-Whining, Be Self-Redefining!

It is vital to holistically re-define and ascertain the emotionally-mental framework of your life every day and night. Even though the mental level is being summarized at the next stage, I want to reiterate the fact that the division of the **SELF-SALVATION** work into cycles in this book, as well as in the previous four levels, helps us assess our progress on this path by ***the analytical work of the left brain.*** The thing is, all the levels are interconnected and inseparable in their holistic frame-work religiously follows the paradigm:

Synthesis - Analysis - Synthesis.

Everything you have become or have not become is no accident! You have been sculpturing your soul either masterfully or negligently. Self-sculpturing requires constant work with your ***"Volitional I"*** *(David Icke),* and it teaches you to follow your will, by constantly looking into the mirror of your soul.

Praise, rebuke, or repel the work of your every day's spell!

Be self-critically swell!

The auto-suggestive work that you are supposedly conducting is meant to help ***you face your inner base with grace***! *(see the book "Self-Taming!" for more)* Synthesize the self-refining process at the emotional level because we are emotional beings, and the way we control our emotions determines the way we build our lives.

Rationalize your emotions and emotionalize the mind! Be One of a Kind!

The ability to put the mind and the heart in sync defines this process and our goal in life is to monitor this process consciously, **INTEGRATING THE FORM AND THE CONTENT** of life to accomplish inner balance that we are seeking. I am sure that just meditating without conscious work at every level is hardly working. A successfully meditating person has done a lot of work at every level We gravitate to the people like that because they magnetize us with their wisdom.

The Physical Form + the Spiritual Content of life = Spiritual Maturation!

The integral process of spiritual maturation never ends, and it is your responsibility to speed it up or to let it slow down, or even stop entirely, letting you go down the apathic road of self-corrode.

Your Life's Fractal Formation is in Consistency and Inner Elation!

8. Self-Reformism Results in Personal Magnetism!

Every person that we come across in life leaves behind his ***informational aura***, or the train of his thoughts and emotions that affect our life and help us either push ourselves forward in the process of our shaping the common future, or he / she negatively impacts our optimism to the point that we let that future stagnate and get bogged up with frustration, fear, doubt, and self-disrespect. ***People either gravitate to us or repel us, depending on the magnetic power that we accumulate***. To consciously perceive the impact of other people on us means to be able to reason out if the soil for the soul is watered by those who happen to be in our lives or dried out by their negative magnetic influence, called **MAGNETIC VAMPERISM**. These people deplete us of energy, pollute our hearts and minds and de-stabilize our psyche. Resist their influence!

So, self-reformism depends of personal magnetism!

It requires a lot of aware attention and intuition processing. *"The hardest laziness to overcome is the necessity to work at understanding the environment and yourself!" (Dalai Lama)* If **the fractal elements of your soul** get negatively affected by the human environment. I suggest you do conscious protecting of your **BODY+ SPIRIT+ MIND+SELF-CONSCIOUSNESS** against any negative disturbance, performing an auto-suggestive inducting then and there. I, for one, immediately command to myself:

Snap out of it! In my thought, I report only to God!

Hopefully, my inspirational boosters and mind-sets will resonate with you, gravitate to your mind, and charge your spirit to help you become more optimistic and self-loving thanks to their ***auto-suggestive afore and afterthought***. I like a wonderful book by a great psychologist *Dr. Paul Pearsall* who writes in his book *"Super Joy,"*

"The joy response to troubles is the essence of the joy of living!"

Steve Jobs also said, *"When you have all the money of the world, you can hire anyone to do things that you need; you can buy any material thing that you want, but there is one thing that you cannot find or buy. This is life!"* Our personal magnetism is built on dignity and personal integrity that manifest the unbreakable unity of the **MIND + HEART** that we need to obtain during the process of *spiritual maturation*, described in the previous books. Don't forget to back up this unity with your unbreakable spirit.

Praying to God Fortifies My Inner Unity Forte!

9. The Threefold Cord is Our Emotional Forte!

(An Inspirational Booster)

To live as a pure man, or a femme

Is not an easy thing to be done!

       Many still stumble on this way,

         With too much dismay!

Spiritual defenses are weakened,

Electronic temptations are beaconed!

       "What do I care?" is heard,

       And the degradation of masses is spurred!

Too much alcohol and drug abuse

Dull our conscience and diminish the patience fuse!

       Youth is smeared by the sex defuse;

     The elderly are pained by a negligence abuse!

  Good judgements are not in fashion,

  People are wearing a crucifix for a sin reduction!

Sinning, though, is booming,

And soul isolation is zooming!

       Chaos is ruling the ball;

    The minds and hearts are in a pogrom! (Russian for a riot)

But if we jointly unite

Against the Sodom and Gomora bite,

Forming with BODY + SPIRIT + MIND "the threefold cord"

According to the sacred word,

We'll prevail and withstand

The common chaos in its stand!

Thus, we'll stop blame-shifting

And start morally drifting!

The chaos will subside

Finally, aside

And in the golden age of hope,

You'll stop seeing your life as an ominous TV soap!

"Our instincts inspire us to look beyond the usual and identify the unusual among the threads of commonality."

(T. D Jakes)

God cannot bless your steps if you do not move your legs!

The banal excuses *"I am a big boy! / I am a big man! / I am a big girl!"* do not work because you cannot act as a teenager one day and a big man another. You need to decide to grow both physically, emotionally, mentally, and spiritually

Life is not what we want. It is what it is!

We need to often go beyond the limits of our responsibilities and *mobilize ourselves for an extra-human effort* if life casts the problem that only a threefold cord can help you overcome.

"The one walking with the wise will become wise" (*The* Proverbs 13:20)

The Forking Reality Suggests
We have Progression in the Consonance Direction!

10. Commit to Being Soul-Fit!

Every one of us has the garden of his/ her soul that is originally planted by our parents and that needs to be taken care of by us with much awareness and care for the rest of our lives. Development of *intuition and aware attention* to life are key here. *"Awareness is always the first step to progress!" (Albert Einstein)* **Try to be always aware of your thoughts and feelings in sync.** In the conflict between the heart and the mind, go after the heart, your intuitive connection to God. The highest union with *the Universal Infinity* happens only if we strive for it consciously and in a holistic unity with life inside and outside.

Create your life's course without any SELF-PITY remorse!

In 1986, an ancient manuscript was found in Uzbekistan. This document was called **"The Code of Secret Knowledge for Future Rulers"**, and it was written in the ancient Farce and Arabic. There were many remarks in its margins. *Dr. Mirza Karim Narbekov* studied this ancient document for years and revealed to us its unbelievable secrets in his book *"Body and the Spirit Training"* in which he reveals the ancient secrets of the physical and spiritual training of a man. I would like to share with you *the idea of the seasonal treatment of a soul* that helps its owner. preserve *the Sanctity of his Being*.

Our souls need inner exploration and spirit formation!

In winter, the soul should be resting, *self-reflecting*, self-cleansing, and self-defining. This is the most important season in terms of a man's conscious self-realization and self-control.

In spring, new seeds of goodness must be planted in your soul with utmost care and accurate choice. *No seed grows without support*!

In summer, the new soul sprouts must have enough sun and be watered timely to grow into the strong plants of *willpower and character.*

In the fall, we are supposed *to harvest the soul qualities* that we had been nurturing and rejoice at having raised our consciousness with their help.

By the end of the year, the result needs to be carefully reviewed and a new round of work at enriching the soul is to begin. So, every soul has to be processed through *cold, warmth, heat, rain and self-assessment* that require our *acute intuition* to guide the process of *soul-refining* consciously.

"Any Human Knowledge starts with Intuition."
(Immanuel Kant)

11. Don't Let Anyone Litter Your Consciousness!

(An Inspirational Booster)

Don't let anyone litter
Your consciousness when you are bitter!

Life is internal
And attitudinal!

We stereotype people and things,
Being unaware of the reasons of their actions' ins!

We adopt patterns from other personas
And make them elements of our own goals!

But the formula, "I think, therefore, I am",
Is only for a thinking man!

Individuals with little definition
Should not change our life's mission!

You must resist their actions' cyst
And lift the veto from our consciousness gist!

Remember, your gut decisions
Are much better than stereotyped incisions!

A person that glitters
Is not all gold in his / her fetus!

Even though everyone
Learns from his own lesson's fun,

God helps only those that help themselves
To remove their life lessons spells!

Here, I agree with David Hume,
"We inhale each other's spiritual perfume!"

So, + be happy for having been born
Human, humane, and intelligently sane!

Let's reverse our Dehumanizing Course!

Let's learn *to be the extra-terrestrially-human*, proud of our compatriots of the Earthly origin, destined to share the time-space on the orbits of space ships and stations with us: *Chinese, Hispanic, Haitian, Indian, African of the American origin, Jewish of the Russian origin, Bulgarians of the Turkish descent, Muslims of the European origin,* **and every other beautiful mixtures of blood in the Universal Blood Flood!** We are different only in the intelligence ration that is our goal on the path of the evolutionary reformation!

Be a Free Thinker!
Don't Be Indoctrinated; Be Self-Liberated!

12. Soul-Processing is in Self-Reassessing!

Aware attention needs to be paid to inner **intuition-based** w**ork of the soul at every level:** *physical, emotional, mental. spiritual, and universal* and in every season consistently, becoming a good. healthy pattern of behavior. The soul will reward you with serenity and self-respect. So, preserve your soul's sanctity.

To be whole, don't forget to lock the gates to the garden of your soul!

Your soul is your private property, your main asset in life! Following Dr. Nabokov's advice, I have been doing self-assessment seasonally for years, and I must admit that such **soul-processing** is self-disciplining in attitude to people of a different skin color, nationality, or religious beliefs. The sense of **self-improvement** is very invigorating because it connects the heart and the mind.

The rainbow of life colors the human tribe!

Aware attention paid to all life on a regular basis helps download our consciousness with new ideas, changed perceptions, opinions, respect for life, and new dreams that change with every new season in full accord with the colorful striptease the life every season.

Life is a kaleidoscope of colors, fill it up with you WOWs!

Our self-image, mood, and most importantly our color-perception of life should be changing with the flow of the seasons. Note, please, that **COLOR-BLESSED** people that pass through our lives beautify it, too. Our differences in skin color are also the **NATURE'S CONTRIBUTION** to the beauty of life that comes in all shapes and colors, like the incredibly-marvelous *life fractals* by Dr. Mandelbrot. Since I came to **this internationally-brewed country**,

I am absolutely mesmerized with the colors in front of my eyes!

So, let's look at each other and see this beauty from inside and outside! Such *colorful perception of life* will help us resonate with the seasonal and weather changes of the Mother Mature in full unity with **the Whole of Life! Our interconnectedness** with Mother Nature, with the animal world, and, of course with the people who pass our path is enriching us with new wisdom. According to science, we use only **5%** *of our brain potential* that is developing exponentially, and we are now trying *to use it terrestrially, extra-terrestrially, and celestially,* tapping into the programs that we are getting from the Universe digitally now. *The Buddhist Mantra teaches,*

"Go Beyond, Fully Beyond, Completely Beyond!"

13. "Love is the Electricity of Consciousness!" *(N. Tesla)*

(The Emotional Dimension of Self-Resurrection - b)

Make Love Ecology Your Personal Psychology!

<u>Create the space of love inside, around you, and Above!</u>

Have Love's Immunity against Evil Impurity!

Auto-Induction:

Emotional Maturation is in Love Elation!

The Life Bliss without Love is a Myth!
(Perseus and Andromeda)

You are Love and Love is Me; We are in Unity!

14. Love is Always an Equation!

(An Inspirational Booster)

Love is always an equation,

Either you love yourself more,

Or the object of your emotional invasion!

       The question" Who is Who?

       Remains a ruling sexual guru!

Either you control me, or I control you

That is the power of " Who?"

       We never forestall

       The fight for the control

It directs, it invades,

It inwardly breaks!

       It is a disease

       Of a de-magnetized "Is!"

Only the unity of you and me

Constitutes the whole without a selfish glee.

       So, tap into each other's interface

       To have an unbreakable love face

Grow into each other's space

But don't occupy it with the Ego's maze!

       The trunk of the Love's Tree

       Consists of two parts - You and Me!

Minus and plus

Make real love, thus !

They are inseparable and unbeatable,

But their love is remittable.

You remit Me, and I remit You,

We are our common love's guru!

Our emotional health

Shouldn't be any shrink's wealth!

We are both in charge to recharge

Our unified cell to love-excel!

And we can monitor our common soul

To love-console!

Love is the Action of Sharing, Giving, and Forgiving!

Love is Our True Being!

Marriage is an inspired decision made with precision!

<u>*The two hearts beat like One only*</u>

<u>*in the space and time of love!*</u>

Are You Spiritually-Fit for the Love Beat?

15. Love Equation Needs Auto-Suggestive Invasion!

The next step on the ladder of ***emotional maturation*** is your heightening the ability to love not just yourself, your loved ones, your parents, kids and friends. Every of five books on Self-Resurrection has the part that presents **_Love is the core of every life domain_**, not only the emotional one.

The ability to love means filling your inner space with grace!

The work at ***the seasonal monitoring of the soul*** that I have briefly described above, should be going on love-wise. The circle of the spiral gets wider as you are moving up, bettering. yourself, level by level and rejoicing at the idea of becoming worthier of life and more loving it in its every manifestation. Remember a wonderful piece of advice the father gives to his daughter in the movie "*The Wedding Planner,*" showing her that love is a process, not an immediate result.

"Appreciation grows into respect; respect growth into like; like grows into love"

The spiritualized intelligence and the **INNER GRACE** that you have accumulated so far spiritually will resonate with your **RAISED SELF-CONSCIOUSNESS.** It will constantly remind you of the ultimate, Universal stage of life that should be anticipated with awareness, inner peace and tranquility. ***The Universal Stage is the stage from which true love always grows.*** That's why when we are lucky enough to meet the soul mate and the feeling of an amazing mutual love generates the butterflies in the stomach and the spirit gets equipped with the wings to fly over any trouble, any distance, any forceful separation, wars, and even death.

Love that starts at the highest spiritual level develops further at the mental one. If our intelligences click, we feel magnetized even more and develop a strong emotional attraction that resonates into the symphony of the physically - uplifting love. Such love energizes and spiritualizes, not diminishes and depletes of energy.

Most importantly, we get inspired to become better for the loved one. We feel happy with what you have accomplished, creating and transforming ourselves at each level on the way to ***Self-Salvation.*** So, focus your **AWARE ATTENTION** on ***the unity of the mind and the heart.*** It is the center of your biological field, connected ***to the Universal Information Field.*** Don't disturb its sacred beat: ***21-21- 21*** or ***Love – Love - Love!***

To Obtain Life Consonance, Get Rid of Love Dissonance!

16. Learn the Main Love Lesson – Every Burden is a Blessing!

Only love teaches us patience, sacrifice, tolerance creativity and exceptionality, up-lifting us over the triviality and harshness of life that never bother those who are pure inside. We call such people *innocence - blessed* because they remain blind and deaf to *the corrupting social immorality and godliness.*

It's hard awfully to be Godly in the godless world!

I would like to remind you here of an ancient parable that is very note-worthy for our re-considering the attitude to life and love that should be **SACRED UNDER ANY CIRCUMSTANCES!** *(Check out the book "Self-Taming"- spiritual dimension)*

Don't be ordinary; be extra-ordinary!

A group of people was building something in the hot summer sun. They were not aware of what they were building, and they did not care to know that. They all looked exhausted, weather-beaten, and very unhappy. Only one man was smiling and singing while laying the bricks. A surprised passer-by asked him why he seemed different and what made him so happy. The man's answer was,

"I'm smiling because I'm not just laying bricks.

I'm building the Cathedral!"

Our awareness of what we are doing in life and why we are doing it makes all the difference! As a matter of fact, **we are building the Cathedrals for our souls throughout life.** Each Cathedral is a resting place to be visited by your soul and other people's souls for a kind word, a sincere expression of compassion, and a welcoming smile.

If you choose to do the seasonal processing of the soul consistently and consciously, your self-assessment and self-boosting will be done in the most inspiring and self-loving way.

Sacredness in Me is what you should always see!

Auto-Induction:

I Make Every Day a Work of Art, so to say!

17. Serving and Giving is the Basis of Good Living!

(An Inspirational Booster)

We break up, make up, or set up

Without thinking twice "What's up?"

    We fall in love with the virtual reality,

      Devoid of any human sanity!

Hence, love goes in reverse

Of its natural human course!

    Men get attracted to handsome males,

      Women prefer frailness to real maleness!

Is it another case of Sodom and Gomorra,

Or should we see it as the saddest umora? (Russian for a sad laugh)

    True, the choice we make, dictate the life we live,

      But the Nature's choice is sacred still!

Are we heading to a total destruction

Of our life-long human function?

    So, let's stop our love rationalization

    And accept or give love without frustration!

Love with, or without a Sex Role Transmission

Is a God-Given Mission!

Love Can Never Cease;

Love is Our Ascending Universal Myth!

18. Develop Love Intelligence Without Negligence!

We need bio-energy to love, to create, to walk, to work, to eat, to breathe and to be joyfully at ease! So, relax your heart and remember to switch your aware attention to *the loving energy of the heart* that needs to be accumulated with self-awareness, self-respect, and constan**t SELF-SCANNING.** Love is a skill that must be developed into the habit *consciously and consistently*. If love life hits the rock, a common practice is to see a therapist. But there is no love space in the heart, and therefore, whatever the advice, it will never cure what's not rooted in the heart.

Love is the seed that is planted into us from birth!

It's every parent's duty to breathe in the space of love into the heart and the mind of a born child and keep watering and nurturing love with sincere care, tenderness, and gentle love always backed up by the best fairy tales, stories about the heroic deeds for love, classical music, and the beauty of the world.

Such massaging of the soul is your every day's goal!

Sex needs to be presented as the most sacred side of life, not a dirty, sinful one, spiced by the askance-viewed sex-orientation. It's the personal and *sacred, taboo choice of the heart,* not the trend to follow, or to blindly judge, without taking the dirty soul's shoes off in public, hungry for your soul.

Sex without love is a Bluff!

Gradually, love gets firmly rooted in the mind and the heart of a son or a daughter. It normally happens during and after the puberty of a human being, and then the sex-oriented minds of our present-day kids will become more romantic and sacredly-protected, not brutally and dirtily-exposed.

Self- education is the basis for love -formation!

The marketing policy - *Sex sells!* needs to be substituted by new, digitally-charged *Love spells help sales!* like the ones, cast at us in the movie *"Her."* The *vibrations of love are being spread to us from the Above*, and our role is to teach ourselves to tune to these vibrations. In the conflict between the mind and the heart, we must always go after the heart, or *our intuitive antenna with the neuro-logical basis* of an unbreakable unit of the heart and the mind.

Love Physiology + Love Psychology = A Healthy Soul Ecology!

Your Happiness Bliss Starts with a Kiss!

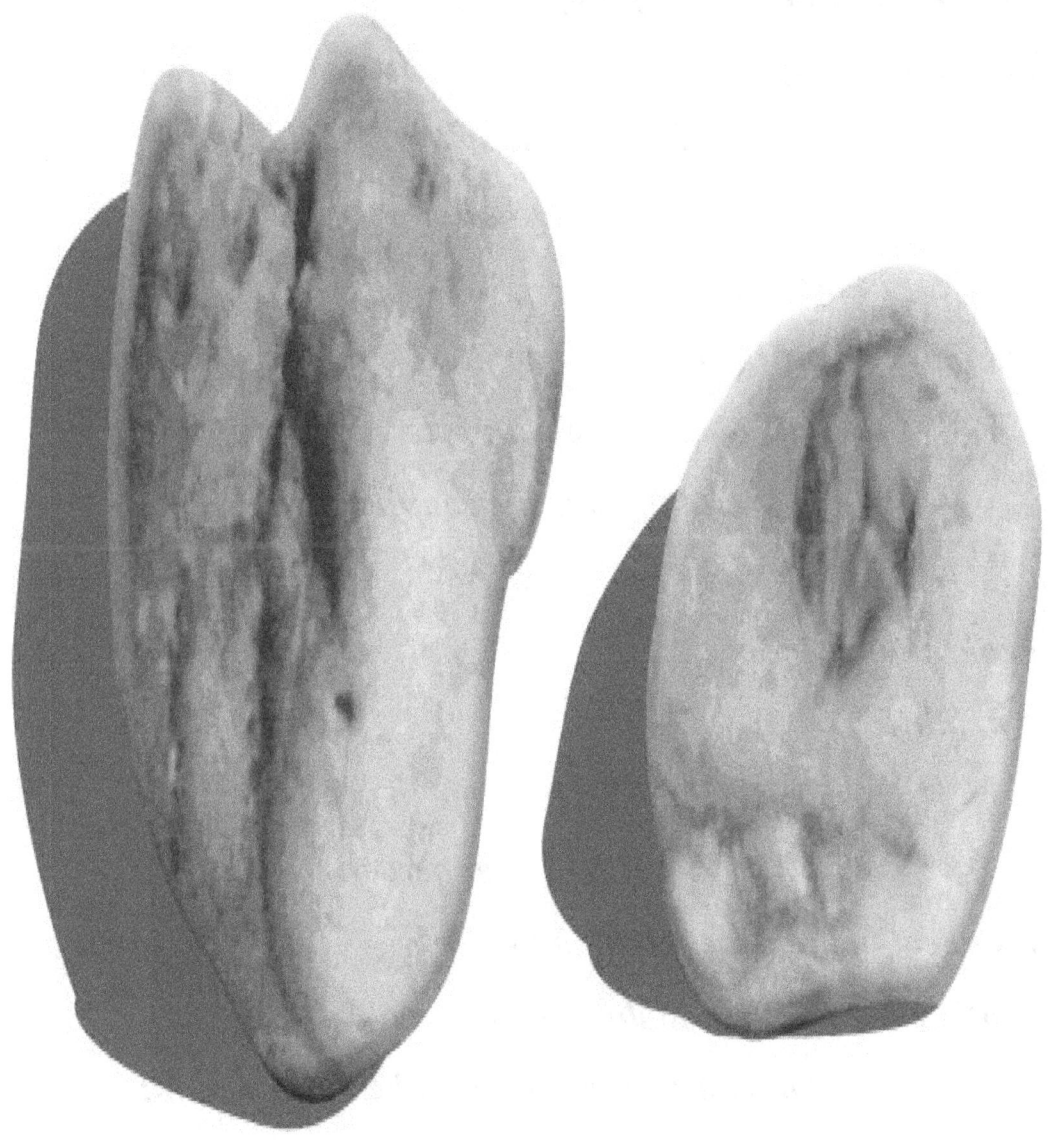

Love is Me; Love is My Philosophy!

Stop feeling pity for yourself, blaming others for your wrong choices and decisions, made in the emotional and mental, dissonance and the broken unity between the hert and the mind. Say auto-suggestively:

You are My Love Goal; I Kiss Your Soul!

19. Meet Your Love Halfway without any Dismay!

To meet someone in love half-way,

Without any dismay,

Is not an easy thing to do

Even for a love guru!

You need to see the eyes

And employ the entire tolerance supplies,

To compromise your interests' striptease,

And to have the zenith of a kiss!

Such consonance in love

Is not a bluff,

And it's possible to achieve

If both can perceive

The love beat of the heart of the other

And that's what you should do, rather!

So, don't be in a fight to be always right;

To be right, be just bright!

Not to break the music of love with a fight cacophony;

Try to always sound as a joint symphony!

To preserve your love,

Tune the soul up to the station Above!

Do not Apply too Much Eloquence,
Better Resort to Patience and Tolerance!

20. Don't Rationalize Love!

(An Inspirational Booster)

When we rationalize love,

We get cut off from the Above

Unfortunately, true Love is leaving our guts,

And it's becoming ugats. (Italian for nonsense)

In the tech era of digital connection,

We get caught in a disconnection

Of our face-to-face inspection

And soul- to- soul reflection

We lose love mentally and emotionally

Because we expose ourselves only partially

Our heart-to hearts and tete-a-tetes

Happen in hasty superficial fits

We read the text messages once or twice,

But we don't see the partner's eyes

Nor do we sigh or romanticize

His or her heart 's size

We are expecting a soul-mate,

But we continue to rate

Every one's love track

By the size of his/ her money sack!

Nor do we want to commit

To a long-term mutual fit.

The Ability to Love is the Self-Denying Stuff!

21. Be Strong Enough to Admit- I'm Not Love-Fit!

(An Inspirational Booster)

Live with diligence

And observe LOVE INTELLIGENCE!

Don't be speech-bubbly,

Recycle your negative vocabulary!

Clean it of the words of profanity,

Complaining, cursing, and vanity!

Also, start reversing

The words of hate into love rehearsing!

The true value of the words heard

Is often twisted into a verbal sword!

That can kill, hurt, and injure

More than any other weapon-like danger

True, life is a "Comedy of Errors"

That are reflected in the God's mirrors

But it would be way less, as such

If we observed LOVE intelligence that much!

And if we became more complemental,

And much less judgmental!

Be kind to the unkind,
And much more of a human-like kind!

So, put your tongue
In the captivity of the mind's run!

And be always on alert
For a LOVE WORD!

Language Consonance destroys
LOVE DISSONANCE!

Be Strong Enough to Admit Your Being Love-UnFit!

"The one who is crooked at heart will not find love." (Proverbs 17:20)

Not to be Starved for Love,
BE A BETTER LOVE DOVE!

<u>Since God is Love,</u>
<u>Our Life Direction is His Love Reflection!</u>

You Can Love Gain Only on the Loyalty Lane!

22. Cleanse the Love Space with the Vocabulary of Grace!

To come to grips with our negative fits and attain **SELF-CONSONANCE**, we need **to X-RAY** ourselves for the negative pests of character that null us out of the productive life in five level: *physical, emotional, mental, spiritual, and universal.* Do it from bottom to top consistently and self- relatively.

"Greatness lies in exceptionalism!" (Jeffrey Kluger)

Habits are akin to addictions. They are stubborn and deeply-conditioned. The only way to handle them is to suppress them *by re-programming your cells and changing the memory hard-ware.* Gradually, such **SELF-SCANNING** will become a good, self-constructive habit that will be backing you up on the roller costar of life fluctuations, *changing the brain's wiring plan.*

Put Yourself in Balance with Self-Consonance!

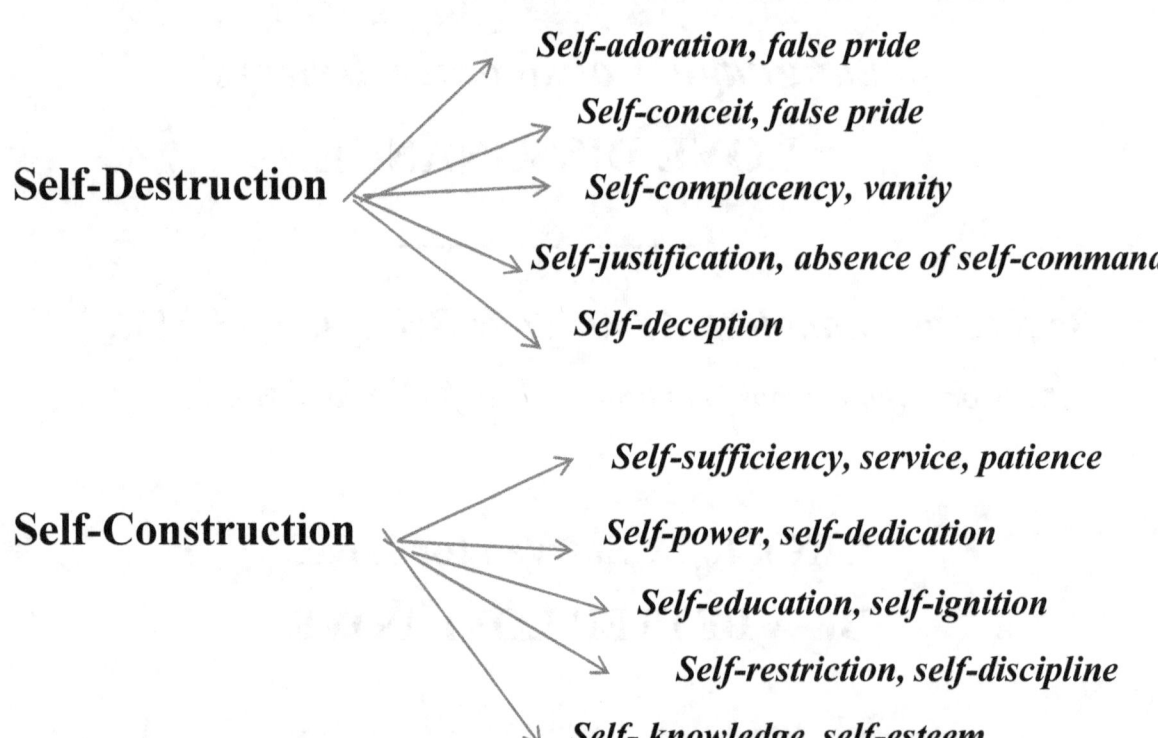

"There is no sadder sight than a young pessimist!" (Mark Twain)

The Beauty of Our Thoughts is in Good Words!

"The one guarding his mouth protects his life." (Proverbs 13:3)

The Language of Love can resolve Any Conflict's Stuff!

23. Get Aboard of the Love Sanctuary of God!

(In Inspirational Booster)

When you are love-distraught,

Pray to God!

    Uplift your spirit aboard

    Of His Universal Fort!

Look down at an angry You

From a bird's eye view!

    Being uplifted by the God's thumb,

    You are unapproachable for anyone

There, you can see

    What you can do

        To save yourself from anyone

        And you!

First and foremost, be sure to forgive

the person who admits his / her fault

and do it without rebuking and re-talking the guilty sort.

Create the Space of Love Inside, Below, and Above!

<u>End of the Emotional Cycle of self- inducting)</u>

Cycle Three
The Mental Dimension of Self-Resurrection!

Sanitize Your Mind; Be One of the Kind!

Cycles of Being

Mezzo level - **Maturation** *(Self-Installation)*

Look Beyond the Prism of Conformism into the Self-Sufficient Individualism!

Don't Be Tribal! Be Cerebral!

The Basis of True Intellectuality is in Spirituality!

"Consciousness is a Creative Force in Action."
(Edgar Cayce)

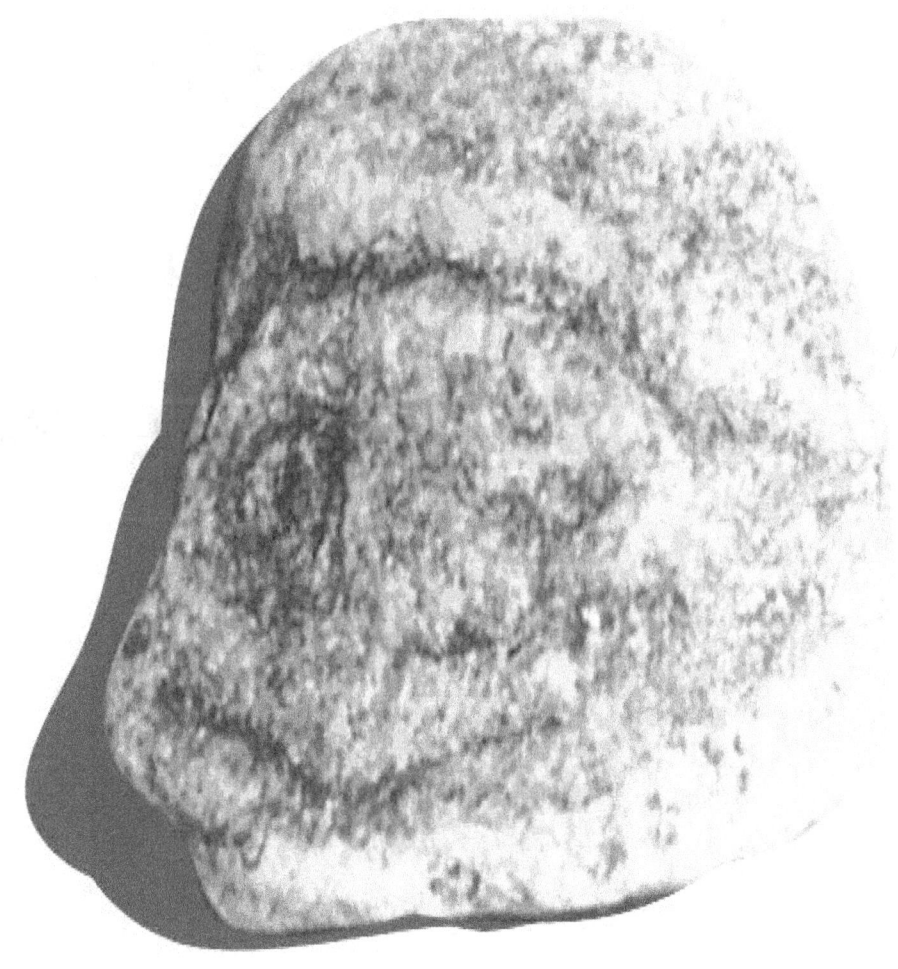

God speaks to us in the Language of Thought Radiation

even in rock formation!

Self-Actualizing means Self-Revising, Working, Loving, Giving, and Wising!

1. Be the Station of Digital Reformation!

To Get to the God's Station, Focus on Intelligence and Dignity Formation!

<u>**I CAN! I WANT TO! and I WILL!**</u>

<u>is your action rule still!</u>

To Be Extra-Terrestrially-Apt, Study the Living Intelligence Art!

2. Consciousness of God is Our Common Mental Fort!

I have noted continuously in the previous four books that *at the Mental Level of Self-Maturation,* true intelligence and *the aristocratism of the soul* start with our comprehending of the creative nature of the Universe and its ruling consciousness. New life awareness demands new **SPIRITUAL TOLERANCE** of the conceptual differences of our definitions of "*God*" under one common understanding of spirituality as the means of connecting to the Universal Intelligence, or *the Consciousness of the Universe* that is sculpturing those who can tune to its signals. *Knowledge accumulation and intelligence take a new meaning at this point*. So, combinatory self-development is needed now.

Self-Transformation is based on Self-Education!

In the book "*Living Intelligence or the Art of Becoming!*" that features the mental level of self-resurrection *(See Book Rationale)*, I present the ways of mind-monitoring through the stages of intelligence development that, on the spiral of self-evolution, we need to raise in five dimensions: **1)** Mini - **Physical level; 2)** Meta - **Emotional 3)** Mezzo - **Mental 4)** Macro - **Spiritual 5)** Super - **Universal).**

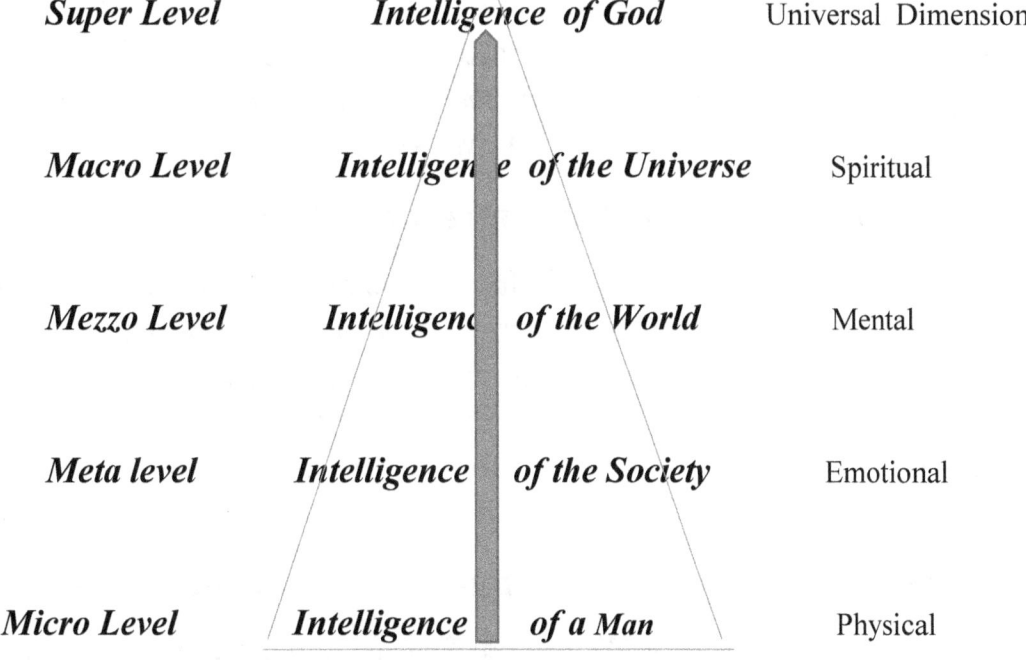

Super Level	*Intelligence of God*	Universal Dimension
Macro Level	*Intelligence of the Universe*	Spiritual
Mezzo Level	*Intelligence of the World*	Mental
Meta level	*Intelligence of the Society*	Emotional
Micro Level	*Intelligence of a Man*	Physical

The last stage in the scale above indicates that *Consciousness is the Universal Mind*, a tiny part of which we are. The self-creation process in five levels helps us *visualize the conceptual structure of life* to channel ourselves on-ward, up-ward, and God-ward!

Intelligence Breeds Self-Consciousness!

3. The Eternal Mind is One of the Kind!

We reflect the Universal Intelligence in our minds if we try to be connected to it through our creative thinking and *conscious and rational perception of life as the time-limited gift.* One thing should be stable and unarguable, though. We need to create ourselves and *uplift our consciousness* every minute, hour, day, month, year in the five dimensions presented above.

The ongoing process **is INFORMATION ⟹ TRANSFORMATION.** It is a never-ending genetic process, modifying our minds and hearts. Only the unity of both makes up our souls, *our eternal mind* – the energy core that is charged with our intelligence and that, in turn, constitutes our growing consciousness through *the ever-evolving fractal structure of the* sacred biological core – **MER-KA-BAH, "THE FLOWER OF LIFE"** *(Drunvalo Melchizedek)* with the center in our hearts.

Mer-ka-bah is the mobile of a soul; it is the soul itself!

It's the electro-magnetic energy of *the mind and heart together*, and the higher a person's consciousness is, the stronger and nobler his soul is! However, consciousness needs to be refined and raised through the process of enriching your intelligence and heart-based, noble actions in life. Check out the ten levels of intelligence in *"Living Intelligence or the Art of Becoming!"* and develop a **FREE-RANGE, UNINDOCRINATED MIND.**

To life-excel, be the best version of yourself!

I do not agree with the founder of Internet seminar *"Mindvalley"* Vishen Lakhiani that states in one of his programs that *"intelligence and hard work have nothing to do with personal evolution and the ability to bend the reality"* for success! For sure, he would never be able *to bend the financial reality and the minds* of those who get magnetized to the idea of becoming successful in life by just meditating and following the subjective information of the author.

Mobilize, don't immobilize your intelligence and the soul's size!

Lock the Gates to the Garden of Your Soul for any subjective mis-information and mis-direction and plant in it the seeds of your own wisdom. **PRESERVE THE SANCTITY OF YOUR SPIRITUAL IMMUNITY!**

Self-Solarize your Soul's Health and its size with SELF-SIFTED knowledge device!

The Light of Reason and Elation is in Self-Education!

4. Consciousness is Intelligence at Work!

Self-assessment, self-education, and constant auto-suggestive work are needed to give your mind food for thought and emotional support that you need to constantly generate *the sync of your mind and the heart*, never losing this connection. Such **SELF-REFINEMENT AND SOUL-RECOVERY** should be monitored by *the blueprint of the intellectual growth* in the mind.

It is paramount to perform weekly, monthly, and seasonal **SOUL-SCANNING** and **SELF-ASSESSMENT** of every level of intelligence across multiple disciplines. (*See the book "Living Intelligence or the Art of Becoming!"*). It will make your self-perfection more goal-oriented, effective, and accurate, fortified by *a* **CONSCIOUS PLAN OF ACTION.**

<u>Holistic life-awareness is needed at the technological time of evolution.</u>

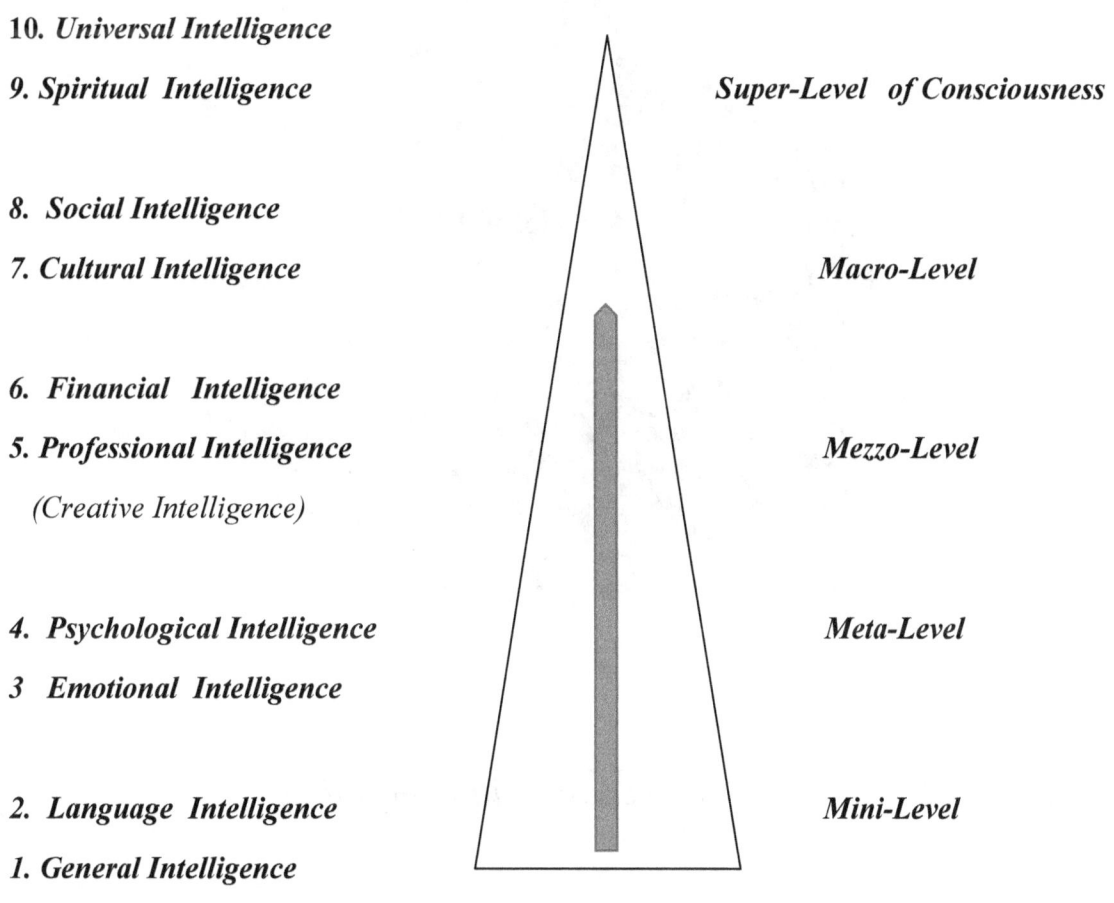

10. *Universal Intelligence*
9. *Spiritual Intelligence* — *Super-Level of Consciousness*
8. *Social Intelligence*
7. *Cultural Intelligence* — *Macro-Level*
6. *Financial Intelligence*
5. *Professional Intelligence* — *Mezzo-Level*
   (*Creative Intelligence*)
4. *Psychological Intelligence* — *Meta-Level*
3. *Emotional Intelligence*
2. *Language Intelligence* — *Mini-Level*
1. *General Intelligence*

If each of us climbs the Ladder of Intelligence, we'll be done with ignorance and negligence!

Knowledge without Thinking Skills destroys the Self-Reformation Wheels!

If You Mind-Sprout,
Life Becomes Your Talent Discovered!

Consciousness is in Everything!

Only with God's Intelligence in Synch
Can We Become What We Think!

5. Self-Education is Crucial for Self-Reformation!

The exponential growth of technology demands that we become more and more insightful *at every level of intelligence -formation because the mental level of self-resurrection precedes the spiritual one.* The level of your education never guarantees that you are in good shape intellectually and spiritually because the scope of our ignorance about life and living is still immense! That's why the prayers of many people are not heard; *there is no proper mental connection established.*

The Internet is an endless source of information, but you need to learn to sort it out for yourself, absorbing only the part of information that you need for the solution of this or that problem. General education is essential in this respect, and the ten vistas of intelligence that I have presented above are pivotal in its formation. New times demand new approaches to the quality of basic education. Thoughtless, uncontrolled work with the redundant information clogs the mind and disconnects you with *the Master Mind* that you need to be in touch with continuously by developing your intuition and constantly tuning up your **AUTO-ANTENNA** *to the Station God - the Universal Information Field.*

Internalizing - Selecting(strategizing)- Actualizing, or Synthesis - Analysis – Synthesis!

The best and the most advanced thinkers among us can establish the channeled connections with the Universal Intelligence via all kinds of meditation techniques, channeling sessions, and the means that teach people to communicate *with the help of telepathy* that, predictably, is going to be our new line of digital connection.

The digitized information then is the liberated spirits of men!

However, such connection can be established only if the channeling person's intelligence is up the par. No wonder, *the spiritual level in the holistic paradigm goes after the mental one.* Any present-day thinker, a philosopher, a guru is always a person of the greatest intellectual capacity that is not just accumulated knowledge. It is processed, analyzed, critically-assessed knowledge that was sorted out from the messy information, and, therefore, it is shining with individual wisdom. The strategic route of such thinking is always the same:

Synthesis - Analysis – Synthesis!

Be Self-Reflective; Put Your Mind into the Clear-Cut Perspective!

6. Form a Brand-New Habit of the Career Growth!

Work on Your Goal by the Paradigm Pole –

Synthesis - Analysis - Synthesis, or
Berth – Life – Death

a) *Generalize and Internalize,*
(Synthesis)

b) *Select and Personalize,*
(Analysis)

c) *Strategize and Actualize!*
(Synthesis)

(See the book " Self-Taming")

Use Your Thinking Time to Business-Ration Your Professional Installation!

7. God's Inkling is in Our Insightful Thinking!

However, *the connection between the mind and the heart* is essential here. We develop bad patterns of behavior because we act under the leadership of the impulsive mind that is always disconnected with the heart in an emotional situation. This is what *slow thinking* is beneficial. This is the thinking with *the insightful support of the intuition* - **INSIGHTFUL THINKING** that is possible only if we take time to listen to both – the heart and the mind.

In the book *"Self-Taming"* that is featuring the spiritual level of the holistic self-development and is coming before this book, I write about **THE WHOLE BRAIN THINKING** that incorporates the left and the right brains, putting the analytical and the creative, synthesizing thinking in one systemic unity that we are supposed to attain in the course of our evolution. Naturally, the development of the thinking critical skills and the operational skills that I describe in detail in the book *"Living Intelligence or the Art of Becoming!"* must be in focus of our education in schools and colleges.

We live the way we think! Both are in an inseparable link!

We are living at the time of information. We have no luxury to stuff the mind with irrelevant information, reading long narrative life, love, or crime stories, or writing diaries. That's not the 19th or even the 20ieth century.

The speed of life requires our constant intellectual and emotional enrichment and soul-refining, not just dining!

But the classic education remains to be the basic education because it reflects the knowledge that makes the mind active time-wise. *This knowledge is the wisdom of the evolution,* the data that every developing mind needs to have in its hard-ware, so that the soft-ware could work selectively and creatively, without wasting accumulated mental energy on dead knowledge or the avalanche of redundant information that creates the jam in the mental traffic. It is very hard these days to have the students focus on the true knowledge.

Insightful thinking needs to be taught and constantly developed!

The information presented in all five books and the boosters, illustrating it will give you some food for thought and inspire you to go to the new levels of self-installation with alert awareness and a conscious plan of action.

To add to the World's Evolutionary Bit,

Be Intellectually Much More Up-Beat!

8. Don't Just Know; Be in the Know!

(An Inspirational Booster)

Knowledge is power,

But it really works only when we empower

The working brain

With love to sustain

The processed knowledge in the wisdom form

That polishes the mind with awareness uniform!

Knowledge is static,

While wisdom is aware and plastic!

The plasticity of the brain

Helps us regain the lost love form again!

Thanks to it,

It's not enough to just know,

We must be

In the know!

It is noteworthy to mention here that **being professionally- aware is not enough**. Employing critical thinking strategies is crucial!*(Check out the book the book " Living Intelligence or the Art of Becoming!")*

"Learning to question our perceptions helps us to resist manipulation and more reasoned judgements."

(Guy Harrison)

"Knowledge isn't What You Know, but What you Don't Know!"

9. Wounds of Intelligence

Healthy, *insightful intelligence* requires also *reviewing our materialistic values* and getting rid **of PRIORATIZING CARREER AND MONEY CHASING** over *spiritualized self-resurrection*. The vastness of the Universal Intelligence is limited by our intellectual laziness that is looming at the time of technological evolution. Technology must be used to develop our intelligence, grow our consciousness, and purify our souls.

Leave the problems into God's hands; solutions are His magic wands!

If we use technology as a supplementary tool in our *conscious time-space relationship with the world,* we'll be able to quicker stop having a merry-go-round life, say no to quick-fix relationships and impersonal attitude to each other, and we'll make inner dignity, honesty, and integrity the base of our souls. So much information is wasted with the consumers in the turmoil of everyday life, and thus, the wounds of intelligence remain unhealed.

Not all knowledge needs to be useful!

Problems sweep us away, and technology is just speeding up their piling if it is used just to automatize and robotize our life. However, only rationalization of life and the use of technology to back up thinking is not enough. Self-scanning in five levels is needed to be constantly done.

Self-assessment and self-reflection heal the wounds of inattention!

Intellectual cooking needs the sorted-out ingredients and aware attention to be paid to the process of attaining the outcome product. *So, stay tuned to new knowledge vibrations and intelligence reformations!* In our quest for the meaning of the new conceptual structure of life, <u>we are learning to decipher the meanings of the universal digital text that is transmitted to us.</u>

Developing our intelligence, **we are constructing new conceptual content of life,** new consciousness of the society and the world, destroying the old ones and using the entropic energy that is released on this path to construct new formations that we are perceiving digitally now.

The information that we are learning to digest is enveloping us as the Universal Intelligence, and that **WE ARE DESCRYPTING IT FROM ONE LEVEL OF CONSCIOUSNESS TO THE NEXT,** inseparable with the levels of our growing intelligence and soul-refinement.

"No Brain – Never Mind!"

The Problem Who comes first - the Chicken or an Egg is still a Universal Puzzle Speck!

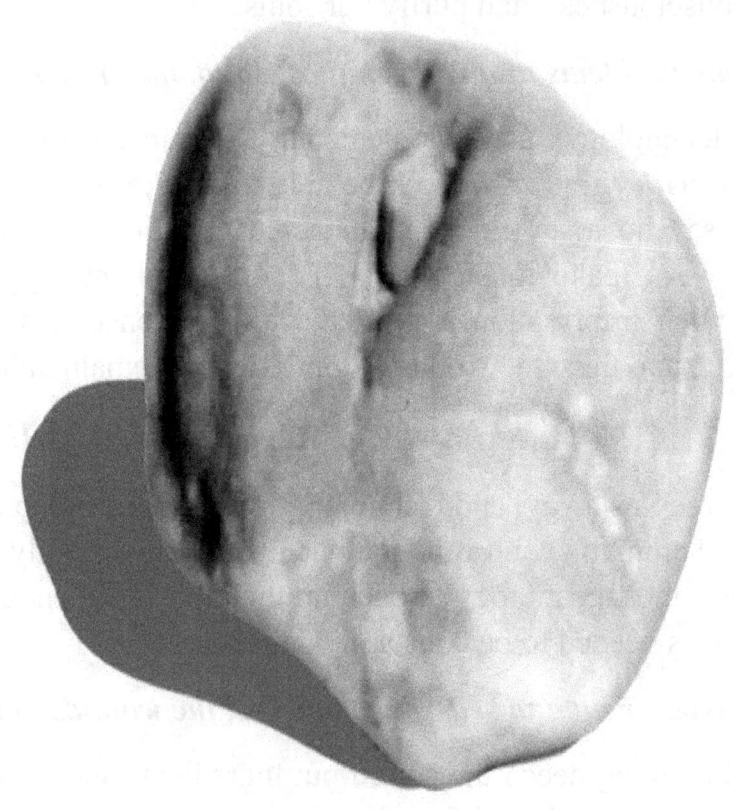

The feeling of total unity makes us deeply aware of the immensity of life in the Universe.

The Life-Determining Bliss is in the Auto-Inductive myth:

I Generate, I Ovulate, I Consecrate My Fate!

10. Self-Revelation is Personal!

(An Inspirational Booster)

Self-revelation is personal,
Self-realization is professional!

Self-management is emotional,
Self-actualization is spiritual!

The channel is directed strictly upward
To the Universal Intelligence and God!

You don't need to have a special ability,
Just visually bridge the reality and possibility!

Also, be always ready to display
The meaning of what you do and say,

For nothing beats
What honesty fits!
Only the developing mind
Gets soul-refined!

Intelligence and Honesty Retention need
Aware Attention!

11. Change the Level of Life Awareness with Fairness!

To uplift your consciousness

Change the level of awareness!

        The last thing you can afford

          Is being a common fort!

Don't think of the physical improvement only,

Work on the emotional, mental, and spiritual bone!

        Optimism is step one,

        Gratitude is step Two,

        Conscious effort is step Three,

   And the aware attention glee

Caps them all with a Worthy Thee!

      So, let the growth of your soul

     Become your prime goal and self-console!

    The growth of our intelligence is directly connected with raising of self-consciousness. In the **Phenomenology of B. Kant,** "<u>experience refers to the experience of consciousness on its way to science.</u>" **Science determines the direction of our thinking**, and we should be physically, emotionally, mentally, and spiritually channeled in this direction!

To Make Your Self-Growth Exponential, Scientifically Enrich Your Personal Potential!

12. To Be Self-Proud, Become Self-Rebound!

(An Inspirational Booster)

To be genuinely self-proud,
Don't follow the crowd!

Go your own unique way
To be devoid of inner dismay

Be an individuality
Without a double-faced duality

Learn to swim against the current,
Obtain your own personal warrant!

Reject, resist, reform
Your inner de-form!

Only then will you become
A truly exceptional woman / man!

So, have a self-pride fest,
And be the Best!

Live in God's Standards, Not in People's Grandeurs!

13. Mind-to Mind and a Heart-to-Heart

There is another very significant point to make here. ***Mind-to-Mind + Heart-to-Heart's Evolution is the Solution!*** Science proves that most of our thinking is done in the perception area. Perception is how we look at things, and how aware of life we are. ***The neurological understanding of the brain affects how we live our lives.*** Our living intelligence absolutely must be enriched with the new insights from neuro-science about the flexibility of the brain and its plasticity. ***Neuroplasticity is an extraordinary discovery of the twentieth century.*** *(Dr. Michael Merzenich*) The development of this innate quality of the brain should be t***he main goal of our technologically-baked up education!*** Such necessity applies to any field of knowledge and any expertise as the demand of our times. ***Knowledge about the brain has huge cognitive benefits professionally!***

We can ***alter synaptic connections in the brain*** and change the language behavior patterns, thus changing a regular human interaction in the ***mind-to-mind communication***, as well as making the interaction with a machine become more and more meaningful in the virtual reality. Also, being right does not mean necessarily that we immediately must find someone who is wrong. "*The finger pointing to the moon is not the moon*". *(Buddha)* Being right means acting with aware attention, applying proactive thinking, purposeful thinking, or the cause-effect thinking that are resisting patterned thinking in its core.

New professional awareness demands conscious recognition of a pattern.

One of the reasons we often must deal with ignorance at work lies in the fact that ignorant people lack intelligence due to their ***patterned thinking blindness*** that is never questioned, challenged, or destroyed with a new flood of consciously processed professional information that demands ***not only a mind-to-mind interaction, but also a heart-to-heart connection,*** and our extra-terrestrial plans can't be accomplished unless we establish a firm connection between the heart and the mind and ***finally learn to listen and to be heard.***

The relationship with our loved ones and the people that pass through our lives only on the mind-to mind basis is good, but not excellent. Only putting the heart and the mind in synch can we get the God's wink of approval, or can we tune ourselves to the vibrations of the Universal Mind that is emitting them non-stop and that the genius of ***Nicola Tesla*** was teaching us to perceive.

Put Your Heart on the Front Seat of the Mind!

End of the Mental Cycle of self- inducting)

Cycle Four

The Spiritual Dimension of Self-Resurrection!

Consonance

Cycles of Being:

Macro Level – **Evolution** *(Self-Realization)*

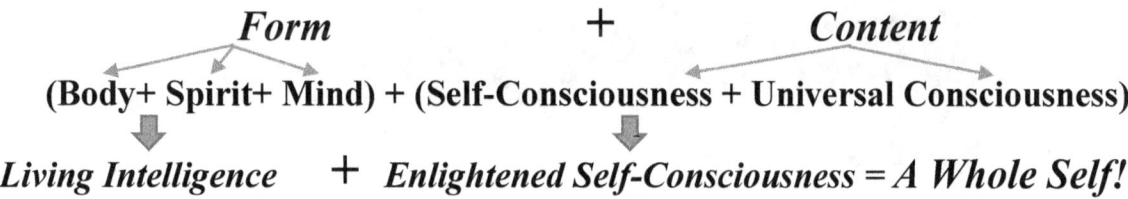

Form   +   *Content*

(Body + Spirit + Mind) + (Self-Consciousness + Universal Consciousness)

Living Intelligence + *Enlightened Self-Consciousness = A Whole Self!*

Life is Both - a Magic Gift and the Product of Effort!

Nothing is Impossible if We Make Our Evolution Irreversible!

To Be on the Evolutionary Porch,
Carry on the Spiritualized Intelligence Torch!

God is Always on the Porch of His Eternal Watch!

1. Try to Live Less Virtually and More Spiritually!

(An Inspirational Booster)

Try to live spiritually

And don't take your problems virtually,

    For as it is Above, so it is below

    Think about it when you feel blue or low.

I am strong in my above ways,

But I am weak in my personal surveys!

    So, now, when something is wrong on my life's track,

    I don't declare this negative fact!

I try to ignore it and disregard,

I am quite good at that!

    I am happy that I am alive

    Healthy, beautiful, and in love with life!

I am also in love with life

For everything below and above!

    Love is my life' load,

    It's my spiritual code!

Thus, I change my spirit's plane

And shape it up again and again!

"Life at its Best is the Life of Faith!" *(Dr. Stanley)*

2. Your Life's Award is in the Spiritual Fort!

Being godly in a Godless world is a real challenge that many of us face now. But if we have an actionable *faith in God – the Universal Mind*, we will continue bettering ourselves from the moment we become consciously aware of a much greater power than us. Unfortunately, many people have been indoctrinated with the idea that if they constantly pray and attend the church, they are developing their spirituality. ***Such faith is blind because God is intelligence in action, creation, and evolution!*** We're all guided by the values, generated by God, but we live by the standards that are shaped by our intelligence and values.

The current values are often self-centered, not God-centered!

All sacred books present the same laws of life that are conceptually illustrated for each one of us with respect to our cultural differences. We, as intelligent human beings, are supposed ***to process the meaning of those laws on our own*** because only an individual person is responsible for his / her spiritual growth, not the priest, not any spiritual authority of any rank, not even the Pope.

"You are your own church!" (*Jesus Christ*)

Jesus Christ, obviously, meant that ***individual processing of spiritual information needs brains*** and a lot of intelligence employed. Jesus spoke in parables, challenging the intelligence of His disciples and the public that was not intellectually ready to perceive Him. For centuries, people got the insightful messages of sacred books individually. Therefore, we have so many interpretations of the Bible and other Holy books. These books need insightful work of the soul.

Processing the sacred word for yourself builds up your inner spiritual cell!

Most evidently, being religious is not yet being spiritual! Churches are mushrooming as businesses around the world; the congregations of religious people are growing, too, but ***the level of our spirituality is hardly raised.*** Why? Obviously, ***underdeveloped intelligence is in the way.*** A person must reason out the concepts of the religious manuals on his own, in whatever amount *Derick Prince* repeated to his followers.

"Your own mind, not mine, is the builder of your spirituality!"

The inner melody of the spiritually-mature people is in synch with the mind. The beat of the heart is rhythmical. They do not allow their instincts guide them; their ***mind + heart connection*** aligns them with the Universal Mind.

You Can Roam any Terrain with God in Your Vein!

3. Christ Consciousness

(An Inspirational Booster)

For centuries on end,
We cannot comprehend,
The spiritual ways
For Christ Consciousness to surface!
The reasons for that are immense,
But the acts of reasoning are in suspense
First, let's learn to go
Beyond the collective psyche's flow!
Individualizing
Means self- actualizing!

Then, we, obviously, need to start
Making kinder a human heart!
Next, we need to release
A lot of anger disease
We still must un-bitter
Very much of our emotional litter!
But we cannot give up
Even on the tiny good stuff
That is left in you, your brother, or a son
Anyone who stretches his hand for a moto-gun
Let's give him or her a conscious bite
And stand up for them very tight!

There is always hope

Even in the worst dope!

There is always some sun

In the puddle of a dirty fun!

All we need to see

Is the soul that has no glee!

It always has a grain

In some deeply buried plane.

We should plant that seed

And let some golden sand to proceed

Then the soul will start to shine

Even if it's tied up with a course twine!

All we need to add

Is some more golden sand!

Grain by grain,

We'll build a castle on this soul's terrain

A puddle of dirty stuff will subside

Gradually aside!

So, every bad guy

Is worth a try!

Every bastard

Can be framed faster

If we give him a chance

At least once!

Even the one with a deadly gun
Can be mentally - emotionally redone!

His damaged soul
Will be consoled,
And he'll move in the direction
Of his soul's resurrection!

Don't be bitter!
Be sweet to reflect the God's light and wit!

Put your "Moon and Sixpence" sides in
synch with the Conscience Might!

Spiritual Maturation is the Inner Music Formation!

Our Spiritual Resurrection is in
Self-Sanity and Much Better Morality!

4. The Spiritual Glee Makes Us Free!

Have you noticed that people with spiritualized intelligence shine from inside, irrespective of their skin color. By the way, since I came to this country, I have met more people with a spiritual glee among the people of color than among the white ones. The main rule of spirituality is observed by them without any compromises and fakeness.

Practice what you preach!

Science proves that true spirituality forms **an aura of protection** for the person of faith. That's why truly spiritual and intelligent people are not prejudiced, black magic involved, or relying on all kinds of predictions. They know the true value of their faith, and it protects them with the glee from inside.

My outside glee is the Inner Me!

Unfortunately, many people go to church every Sunday, sing and pray socially, but their souls are dirty, indifferent, and lacking compassion. They stop appreciating life in its authentic essence, and they are too preoccupied, displeased, discontent, and angry to see the beauty of it around.

"At a certain point in life, most of us quit puzzling over every day phenomena. We might savor the beauty of a blue sky, but we no longer bother to wonder why it is that color." (The Science of Creativity,2018).

We are rarely perfect in what we do, but, irrespective of the fact whether you have been very consistent in **the process of the conscious rationalization of your life,** or less so, do not lose the perspective of self-bettering. Remind yourself,

I have built my inner sanctuary as the retreat from being life-beat."

You are building **your own Cathedral** and allow me to help you lay some **inspirational bricks** to it to help you make it more stable, solid, and indestructible. Continue self-inducting yourself for any goodness that is innate in all of us.

Your being the best will always manifest!

Let's **build up the spirit level by level**, starting with the physical dimension, going up the emotional make-up, constantly refreshing the mental frame-work, and spiritual enlightenment, as a never-ending work on self-inspiring and filling your inner sanctuary with light and love.

"As it is Above, so It is Below!"

5. On the Path of Godliness!

I am radiating Light
To You,
And you are radiating light
To Me!

Together we accumulate
The Spiritual Glee
That illuminates
You and Me!

"Every one of us is either a Clear Vessel of Light, or a Stuffed Vessel that needs cleaning."

(Edgar Cayce)

6. Raised Self-Consciousness
Propels us On-ward, Up-ward, and God-ward!

On the Path of Godliness,

Don't Turn away from Other People's Problems!

Be a Good Human Kind – One with the Universal Mind!

7. The Process of Spiritual Hygiene!

The process of spiritual hygiene
Is going on in your terrestrial gene!

To capture the essence of living,
Insert an inspirational virus into your being!

Make light your personal sight,
And let the godly might stay inside!

According to the Law of Compensation,
Inner light will fill you up with elation,

And you'll be able to shout,
"I have my talents discovered!"

You'll also beat the competition of the 666
And balance yourself in a solid 999 fix!

Thus, you'll nip in the bud
The festers of your gut!

Self-Induction:

"I Illuminate and Elevate My Fate!

8. To Be on the God's Porch, Build up Your Own Inner Church!

Christ said under the disciples' hungry watch,

" On this rock, I'll build my Church!"

And so, I do,

Building up my church inside myself and you!

The rock of your self-worth

Is here on Earth,

And your church will sit

On the top of it!

Your thoughts and feelings

Make up your congregation dealings.

You are the formation

Of your own obligation!

But your church can exist and prosper

Only on the brick of the sacred Gospels!

So, visit your church as often as you can

To prolong your spiritual life span!

Commit to God on the porch

Of your personally built church!

Auto-Induction:

In My Thought, I Report Only to God!

9. Souls Do Not Die; They Spiritually Survive!

As it was noted in the book *"Soul-Refining"* (*the emotional dimension*) that souls go beyond the terrestrial boundaries up there somewhere because they are not separate entities. They are part of the whole – *the Unified Field of Energy* that we all came from, to begin with.

After a person's death, the soul of a diseased man is pushed up by the strong mental energy of the mind only to get back in a transformed way later.

Intelligence and energy, or idea and matter in sync govern this eternal process on the life's rink.

If we try to go beyond our bad habits, conditioned, automatized thinking, our materialistic values, and other imperfections, the soul that is known to be immortal will become *a holistic symbiosis of matter(energy)* and *intelligence (idea)* that is *harmoniously integrated by the Unified Information Field.*

Life can never be stable and happy all over. It is meant to be based on up-down vibrations, minus and plus, order and chaos, destruction and construction, evolution and entropy, or God and devil at large. Our polarized perception of life demands that we unify our differences, take life **AS IS,** and appreciate its happy and unhappy moments as the given.

Self-transformation is based on self-elation!

Self-suggesting, in this context, or *self-hypnosis* appear to be much more effective than affirmations, quotes, or just interesting sayings. Rhyming, self-suggestive boosters also help *resist mental slavery of stereotyped thinking* and acting on the automatic pilot that needs either an authoritative command of the mind, or a nice reminder about inner balance emergency.

Auto-inductions should be up-loaded into the mind for the cases of immergence. You may pick the most appealing mind-sets to you, and down-load them into your smart phone. The popping of the right mind-set in front of your eyes at the right time will calm you down, add confidence, and help you make the right decision.

We must be training the mind against self-perpetuality of life and the negative force fields, and self-suggestibility is the only method that can help us make order out of chaos and make beautiful music our of ugly, soul-destructive noise. This book is a modest attempt to present the methodology by which we can inhibit our automatic thinking and the disintegration of our souls.

Life is an Enigma, devoid of Consciousness Stigma!

10. Delete the Evil with Your Spiritual Upheaval!

(An Inspirational Booster)

So, learning to thank God for the life's hell,

We immediately remove the evil spell!

The lesson gets learnt,

And the balance of life is returned!

Thus, the heaven and our heling

Are only in our polarity dwelling!

If we remove it from our divided minds,

Life will get into the universal twines!

We'll able to resist

The evil spirits' twist!

The music of life will fill us up with elation

And a true life-loving inspiration!

Then, the Temple of Solomon

Will get built in our Inner Unified Form!

So, heighten your life awareness,

And be the pool of Consciousness!

Resist, Reform, and Reject
The Smallest Evil Speck!

11. Don't Be Color-Blind; Be Color-Refined!

(An Inspirational Booster)

God's brain is One

In the universal color-skin span!

      We are One in His brain;

    We are all unique in His domain!

We do not choose to be black, yellow, or white,

So, why do we fight?

      Why don't we abstract

        From the centuries of this whack?

Let's reverse

The perception of some human moths!

      Let's rewind

    The history of our imperfect mind!

And Unite as One Cell

In the Vast Universal Spell!

The Humanoids are Noted to Be Dark-Skinned. Isn't that a Good Hint?

12. Give Your Brain a Conscious Reboot!

(An Inspirational Booster)

Stereotyping stimulates unthinking;

Following a multitude is against God's Inkling!

How can One

Encapsulate all the info-fun

And reboot his inner brain's shit

To a non-tendentious wit?

One needs to crack the usual unconscious code

And start thinking in a conscious mode!

Then, the unfathomable cognitive process of yours

Will be channeled away from the human moths!

And your uniqueness

Will outshine the common materialistic bleakness!

Put Your Soul's Make-Up Under the Thinking Cap!

"Wisdom Outweighs Any Wealth!"
(Sophocles)

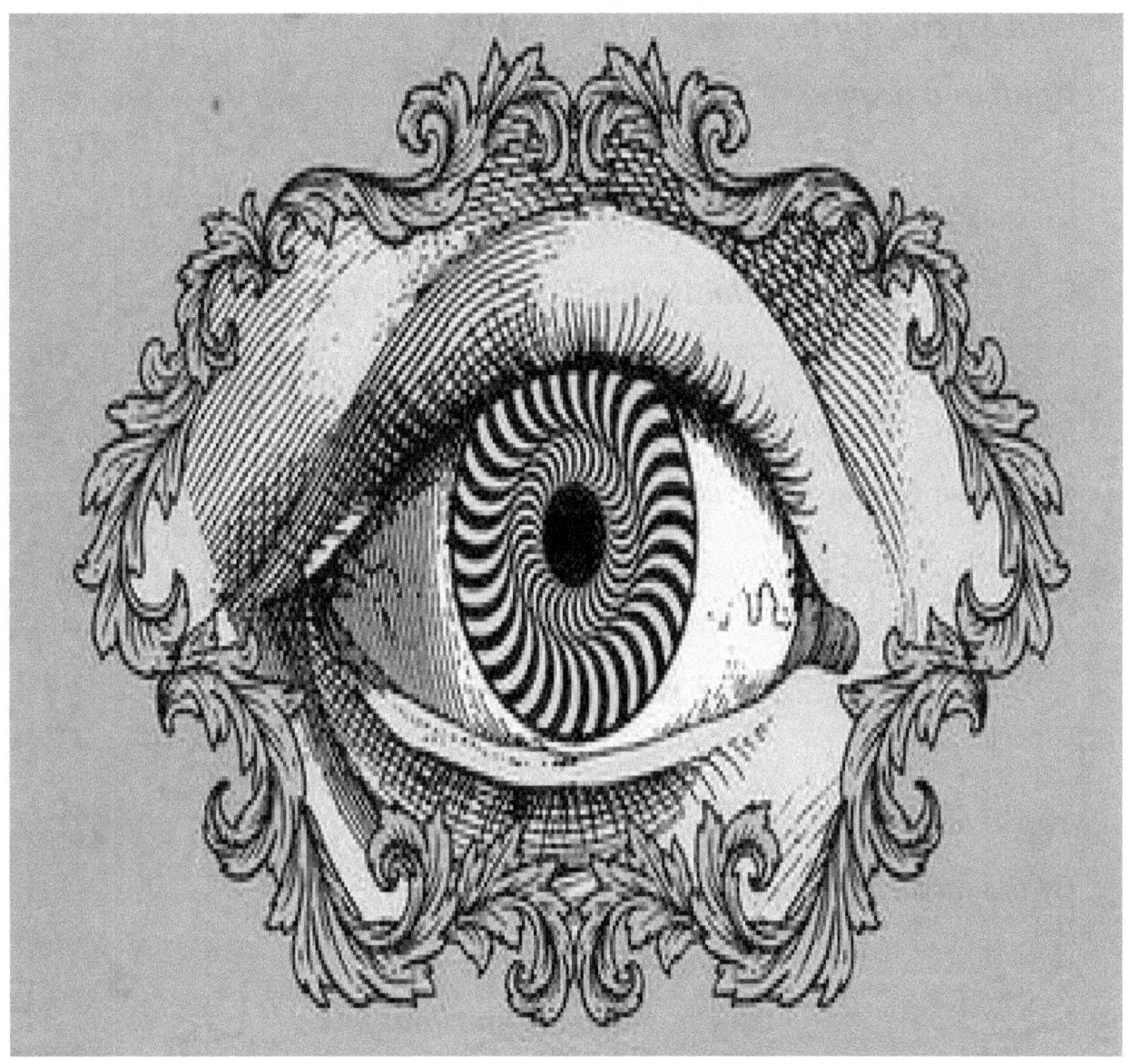

The Chechen Eye of Wisdom

The more God you have inside,

the more happiness resides outside!

Life in its Entire Mass holds Lessons for us!

13. Make Your Spirit Rewire, Uplift, and Inspire!

(An Inspirational Booster)

Make your spirit rewire,
Uplift and inspire

You and your messy thoughts
That ground you with their infectious warts

Cloak yourself in light
And have God at your side

Everything will burn out
In the violet light on that route.

You'll become clean
Of the torturing you sin.

You'll get to the spiritual fort
Of the Almighty God!

Up-load the majestic and soul-refining music of Bach into your smart phone. It will enrich your soul with **the aristocratic tone!**

Be a Stoic not for fun,
Get though life with an Uplifted Thumb!

14. Honor Yourself to Honor Others!

(An Inspirational Booster)

Loving is honoring
 And God-following!
  It's a habit that needs to be instilled
   From the moment you get born, indeed!
Any time of your soul's awaking
Is good for your bad habits' breaking!
  Negligence and disrespect for oneself
   Resonate in another person's cell!
 And our inner magnetism
Gets blocked in its own "ism!"
  By removing egotism,
   We follow love-honoring sophism

  That's based on honesty which can always beat
  Your dishonored self-defeat!

"If I see, I will believe. "Believe, then you'll see."

Make Time for Being Happy,
Not Snappy!

15. Be the Spiritual Station for Love Inspiration!

(An Inspirational Booster)

Be the station
For love inspiration!

Admiration with love
Is our common stuff!

So, have a conscious stay
At your love bay

Revitalize your mind,
Become love - wise, and kind!

Change your hate mood
Into the love food!

"The best remedy for a man's life is love and care.
What if it doesn't work? - Enlarge the dosage."

(Anton Chekov)

Make Loving and Forgiving the Working Rule of Living!

16. Be in the Sanctuary of God!

(In Inspirational Booster)

When you are distraught,

Pray to God!

Uplift your spirit aboard

Of His Universal Fort!

Look down at

An angry You

From a bird's eye

View!

Being uplifted by the God's

Thumb,

You are unapproachable for any

One

There, you can see

What you can do

To save yourself from anyone

And you!

First and foremost, be sure to forgive the person who admits his / her fault and do it without rebuking and re-talking retort.

Create the Space of Love Inside, Below, and Above!

17. I Am the Infinity in Action!

(An Inspirational Booster)

I am the infinity in action,

I am tranquility in motion;

        I am the sea,

        I am the ocean!

I realize my thoughts

Though the well-chosen words!

        I govern my emotions

        And control my devotions!

I never lose the sight

Of my divine might!

        So, be it, as it may

        In the Universal World of no dismay!

Even though life might not be taking you into the extra-terrestrial realms yet, keep flying in your mind.

    "Beyond, fully beyond, completely beyond!"

A famous proverb ***"The birds of feather flock together"*** is, in this case, about the like-minded people, like you, who are exploring the extra-terrestrial vastness of knowledge and give food for thought to their imagination.

    "Knowledge is limited, imagination is limitless!" *(Albert Einstein)*

Time is Gliding on, and it's Great to Have Been Born!

(End of the Spiritual Cycle of self-inducting)

Cycle Five
<u>The Universal Dimension of Self-Resurrection!</u>

<u>Be</u>
<u>a Human</u>
<u>Angel!</u>

Cycles of Being:

The Super Level – **Dissolution** *(Self-Salvation)*

I Am You, and You are Me - We are in Unity!

The Universal Dimension of Life is for

Our Unification and Self-Salvation!

Prefer Eternal Flying to Common Dying!

"I am an Angel!

"We are born with a cry; we die with a moan. What's left is to live with the laughter's bone!"(Victor Hugo)

Synthesis- Analysis- Synthesis!

Life – Death – Life! Go Beyond Survive!

1. Accept Your Life in its Entire Mass, For it Too Shall Pass!

Life is Just a Moment Of Our Dissolution In Everyone and Everything As a Gift of Self-Solution!

Ascension of consciousness from negativity to positivity is slow but sure, and nothing should hinder its de-tour!

Thank you, God, for your Blessing and My Life's Processing!

Even **the medical symbol, the Caduceus** has the image of two serpents, winding around a winged staff, symbolizing the raising of consciousness on the pole of evolution. The wings of the snakes, personify our dream to rise beyond the banality and irregularity of life. The caduceus is, in fact, a symbol of our spiritualized wisdom!

Wisdom is Me; Wisdom is My Philosophy!

2. The Process of the Universal Hygiene

(An Inspirational Booster)

We are becoming more and more informed
About the process of the universal hygiene that is being formed!
The seeds of our knowledge domain
Grow into the grains of wisdom main!
We are learning to manage the subconscious
By getting in charge of our conscience!
More and more of us merge
With the aware attention search!
With it, we better perceive
The universal reality scene!
We started to see. talk, feel, and think
With the Universal Mind in synch!
The sense of self-responsibility
Is electrifying our inner utility!
We learn to go beyond our expectations,
And we speak with less and less negations!
We get mentally charged with "LIKE BEGETS LIKE,
And the link with Higher Conscio
usness gets a new energy spark!
Our hearts become smart and the minds kind,
And we are turning into extra-terrestrial kind!

So, to Enjoy the New Life's Glee, Learn to Live Consciously!

3. I Am God and God is Me! We are in Unity!

Finally, in the Universal Dimension, you can round off the five steps of your self-creation: *Self-Awareness, Self-Monitoring, Self-Installation, and Self-Realization. Keep* sculpturing yourself in five dimensions consciously and in an inseparable unity with all life around you. *Appreciate your life in time and space.* Remember that people who are living at your time and in your space are your contemporaries. The things, pets, animals, trees, insects, etc. are the part of your life and death, too. Do not endanger their life. *Respect it knowingly!*

Stay connected through your **AUTO-ANTENNA,** your intuition, **YOUR HEART AND MIND IN SYNC,** to the Universal Mind and be with it as *One of a Kind! Disconnection is death!*

Form + Content = Holistic Self-Development!

	Super level	**Super-Consciousness**	*Self-Salvation*
	Macro level	**Self-Consciousness**	*Self-Realization*
	Mezzo level	**Mind**	*Self-Installation*
	Meta level	**Spirit**	*Self-Monitoring*
	Mini level	**Body**	*Self-Knowledge*

<u>*Body+ Spirit+ Mind + Self-Consciousness+ Universal Consciousness*</u>

= A New, Holistically- Developed You!

God is Me, and I am God!

God is in me;

   God is with me;

God is for me;

   God is Me!

       God is everywhere I go;

       God is everything I do;

       God is everyone I meet;

       God is all I need!

<u>God is One with Me; God is Me!</u>

4. Equip Your Life's Watch with the Digital Torch!

(An Inspirational Booster)

Creativity is heaven, destruction is hell,

We all know that very well!

        But just to know

        Is not enough, though!

We also need to be digitally-fit

To get much better aware of it!

        Because heaven is our cognitive creativity,

        While hell is a self-destructive infinity!

We need to stop talking with negation,

And start living with constructive elation!

        "It takes only a stroke to change a minus

        Into a plus", and be constructive, thus!

Your thinking transforms,

And it stops accepting the negative forms!

        We gradually realize that the hell

        Is hidden in our emotional cell!

Since God is ruling the world, and that is true,

He oversees the hell in you, too!

Our Better Perception of the God's World

Teaches us to see the Self-Created Underworld!

5. The Law of the Right Human Behavior,

Life proves that *we need broader moral scruples,* and we should not compromise them. They always live in sync with *the Law of the Right Human Behavior,* and, therefore, such people are much happier in life. Inner gravity keeps us on the right track. *(See Richard Wetherill, "Right is Might"),* and their minds are rarely thrown off the paths of *"pure reason"* *(B. Kant)*: ***"Think, say, and do right!"***

Auto-induction: ***Inner gravity is my sanity!***

Such people are not afraid to make mistakes because they are keenly conscious of the causes of those mistakes, and it does not take more than one repetition to make the lesson clear for them. See the ***Parable of Christ,*** in Part Three, 2.

"A person needs to be afraid only to the extent that he is wrong."

You are the writer of your own life story. Having formed the self-image does not mean that you are done working on yourself. It is a non-stop process that requires ***constant self-assessment in terms of the right and wrong perception of your actions.*** You need to take an honest **OBSERVER POSITION** in life, trying to be aware all the time at what stage of self-creation you are.

Nothing beats what honesty fits!

***One more self-demand is essential.* TALK LESS!** Do not spill hard-gained grains of wisdom and intellectual maturity. Substance in thinking and talking shapes you in the best way possible, gives you food for thought, and instills self–respect in yourself.

Auto-induction: ***Start talking less but thinking more; that's the Law!***

Switch from superficial conversations to substantial ones! Soon negative images of doubt and fear that haunt us and that people are in a hurry to share will never happen. ***Your intuition will prompt only positive things to you***. Through talking less and thinking more, you will be able to center yourself in any situation. ***You are not a human moth; your own boss!*** There is the proverb in Russian that tells men when choosing a wife to pay less attention to how she looks and consider the way she talks.

Sincerity is the strongest charm of any femme!

When the Mind is Cultivated, Your Life is Regulated!

6. Fill Your Inner Soul's Cavity with Personal Gravity!

We all have the intuitive guidance that teaches us *to read into the coincidences* that occur to guide us in the right direction. You will be aware that each time any coincidence occurs, it leads you into something new. You will learn to enjoy life despite many unsolved problems, following these Universal leads.

People with aristocratic gravity should be the etalon of our sanity!

In contrast, the people who are dominated by the external factors of life are weak, reactive, programmed, dependent, and emotionally unstable. ***They are scripted by other, much stronger people.*** There is ***no inner gravity*** in them to sustain their own course of action. Don't let anyone script you! Be aware and alert to the others' ruinous intrusion! ***Screen the negative vibrations!*** Once you know who you are and in what department you need constructive, deformational work to be done, you will ***stop justifying yourself*** for the mistakes that you had made in life and start learning from them, never making them again.

Auto-induction: *My inner gravity always works for my sanity!*

Like *the Cosmic Law of Gravity* is monitored by the Universal Intelligence, your ***personal gravity has the mental magnetic force***, too. It is called **WILL-POWER**, and it is ruling your inner world against any habitual patterns of behavior. I'll quote Albert Einstein again because it always resonates with my students:

"Bad habits have a good tendency: either you kill them, or they kill you!"

The inner gravity that you are focused on developing will help you stay away from any bad action, any wrong doing, any temptation and ***demagnetization of your spirit***. *(See the book "Self-Taming!"- the spiritual dimension)*

The piercing eyes of Jesus Christ will be your point of reference.

The process of inner demagnetization is very common nowadays. It is demoralizing many people that never even ask themselves the question, *"Why do I live? What's my mission here? What is right or wrong?"* Eventually, they stop caring, and it is very dehumanizing. Far too often we hear the phrases: *"I don't care!" "What do I care?" "I care less!" Whatever!"* These statements are extremely harmful because their negative suggestive power gets rooted deep in the brain, and we reap what we sow. Limitless carelessness is all around us!

Surpass Yourself with the Morals that are Celestial, not Terrestrial!

7. Beware of the Common Conformity Wear!

(An Inspirational Booster)

Common conformity

Is the problem of people's deformity!

But the dominion of true learning

Must remain one's own personal yearning!

So, let's make life less consequential

And much more wisdom-potential!

Then our life mal-practice will subside

And the God's lessons will get inside!

We'll stop categorically-assessing

What God is processing!

And our independent thinking

Will get in synch with God's inkling!

Begin every day with the victory over your laziness,

fear, and carelessness!

Avoid a Comparison Trap;
Be in the Unique Yourself Wrap!

8. If Imported, Vices Can Still Be Reverted!

(An Inspirational Booster)

Nothing is ever static,

And life is not graphic!

   Both vices and virtues can be reverted in size,

    If your conscience becomes ethicized!

Any addiction can be enticed,

Or better demagnetized!

    Breaking up of the will

     Is also not a standstill!

To just remove the troubling sore,

You have to will your life more!

   Then, "The Catechism of the Council of Trent"

    Will become our common trend!

Thus, your praying will be morally-enhanced

And consciously - revised in your prayer twice:

   "Dear God! Make me invincible to evil

    To burn it down and de-evil!

Live for Your Greatness, Not Bleakness!

9. As Years Go By...

(An Inspirational Booster)

As years go by, we must abide
With the measure of our every day's bite!

We need to accept, appreciate, and act
With the life's pace in tact!

We must watch consciously the life's pulse
And never forget to say, "Thank You," thus!

Breathe in gratitude,
And breathe out attitude!

And with this strategy in mind,
The heart will get in touch with the mind!
Weakness and negligence will subside
And harmony will start ruling the broken inside!

"There are six best doctors for you to consult: the Sun light, rest, exercise, diet, self-confidence, and true friends."
(Steve Jobs)

Never Stop to Create Yourself in the Life's Web Cell!

10. The Fractal Formation is Life's Identification!

Our Fractal Formation is in the DNA Indentation!

Body + Spirit +Mind + Self=Consciousness + Super-Consciousness = The Integral You!

WE are all of One DNA in the Universal Bay!

11. The Way People Treat You, God Does!

(The Inspirational Booster)

The way people treat you, God does!
This is how He rejects or accepts life in us!

"Treat others as you want to be treated yourself"
Should be engraved in our every cell!

Respect, tolerance, patience, and self-control
Must be at the top of our human moral!

Be governed by love in every situation
Fill your mind and heart with elation!

Don't be under-developed, uncivilized,
And immoral and un-humanized!

Form the center for love rating
By way of your mating

With yourself, your partner, and the Son
As well as everything under the Sun!

Most Importantly,
Mate with God Permanently!

12. Believe God, Not Just in God!

(An Inspirational Booster)

I declare it to be the wrong word
To just say, "I believe in God!"

> *The one must say*
> *Without any inner dismay,*

"I believe God helps me in what
I accept as His reward!"

> *When we believe God, but not in God,*
> *We decipher the Universal Code!*

We discard the doubts,
Or any one's planted sprouts,

> *And we get connected to the Master Brain,*
> *Because our life gets in its protective domain!*

The prayer must be your first action, not the last reaction!

Let's Propel the Awe of Thought and Believe God!

(End of the Universal Level of self-inducting)

13. Self-Blessing is Life-Obsessing!

(The Prayer to God for the Everlasting Support)

Teach me, God,
To have the sight,
Teach me to tell
The wrong from the right.

    Teach me, Father,
    To sing and to dance,
    Teach me to appreciate
    The once given chance!

Teach me to share
What I begot,
Teach me to dare
What I haven't got!

    Teach me to live
    In the Now,
    To break the strains of the past
    And get the future skills of "How?"

Teach me to love
The entire life,
Teach me to cherish
Every day and night!

    Teach me to serve
    On the mission of Love,
    So, I could receive
    The grace from the Above!

Love is Me! Love is My Philosophy!

Conclusion of the Inductive Self-Infusion

The Universal Level of the Existing Life Fort is Overwhelmingly God!

(The Call for the Unification in Spirit!)

Let's come to terms with the Virtual Reality - the back-ground for our Spiritual Sanity!

Only with God in the Extra-Terrestrial Sync, Can We Become What We Think!

Life is the Reflection of Our Inner Perfection!

Don't Deform the Consonance of Its Content and Form!

1. Strategizing Your Sight Determines Your Life's Might!

The Universal Consciousness is ruling the World and You in it, too!

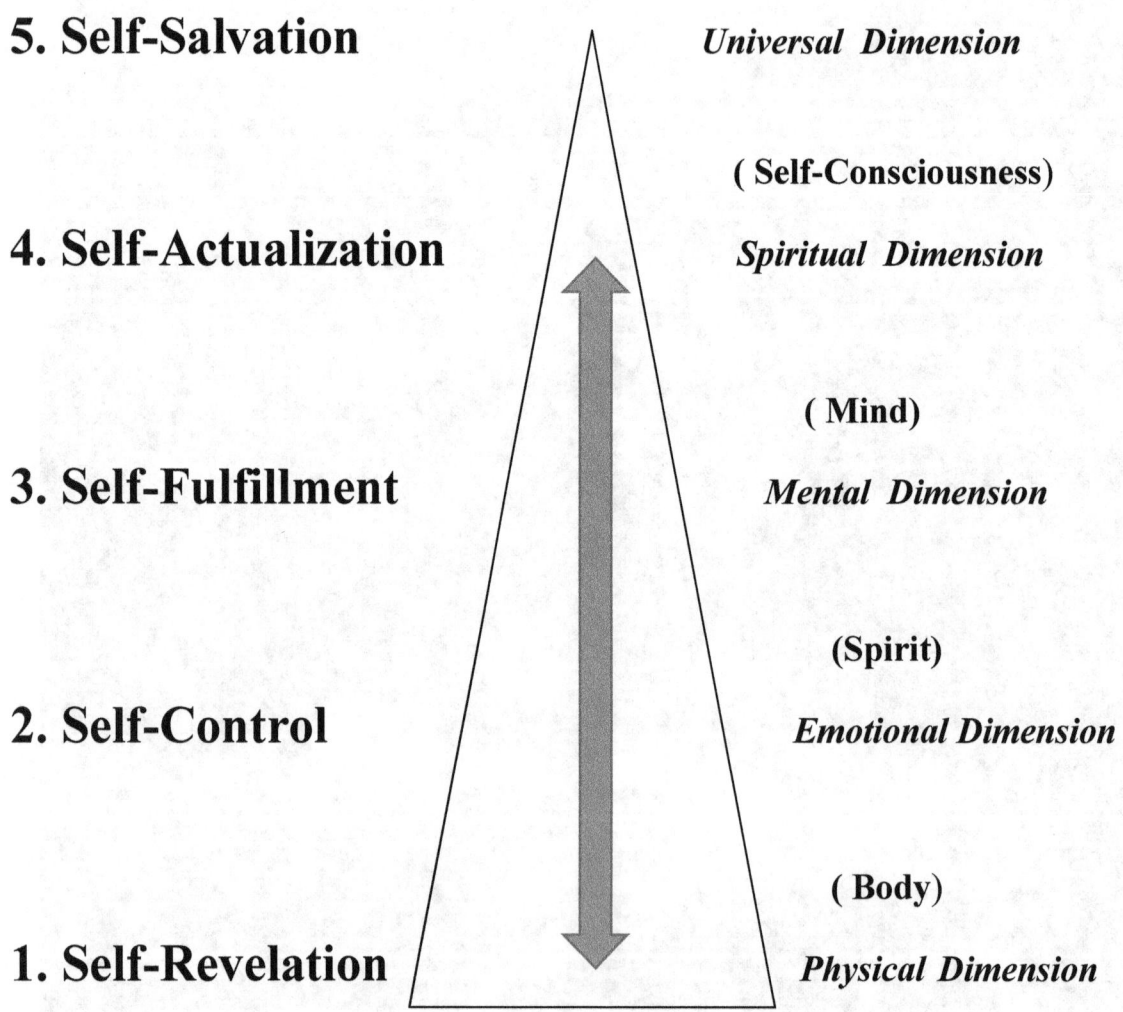

5. Self-Salvation		*Universal Dimension*
		(Self-Consciousness)
4. Self-Actualization		*Spiritual Dimension*
		(Mind)
3. Self-Fulfillment		*Mental Dimension*
		(Spirit)
2. Self-Control		*Emotional Dimension*
		(Body)
1. Self-Revelation		*Physical Dimension*

The Spiritual Fractals of Being:

Body + Spirit + Mind + Self-Consciousness + the Universal Consciousness = A Soul-Refined Self!

Self-Salvation is in Our Spiritual Maturation!

2. Develop Yourself Holistically, Not Mystically!

To be in accord with God, develop yourself holistically in five levels of what is overwhelmingly God! Keep self-affecting and self-reflecting!

Learn the Art of Living and Becoming!

First, in the Physical Department - "Know Thyself!"

*Learn to watch, trust, and respect your body. The body talks to you in **the language of intuition and pain.** Listen to it and respond to its messages timely and consciously.*

It's hard to live with self if you do not know yourself!

Be intuitively tuned to every organ and communicate with your cells while meditating, programming them for health and unity with your immortal soul that you need to continuously develop and enrich consciously, programming and re-programming your cells, your mini-computers

Your cells are the people of your bodily estate;

keep them happily innate!

Second, in the Emotional Department, you absolutely need to be emotionally-equipped!

To begin with, learn to tame *your tongue* because language is the level of ("First was the Word!"), and make it follow the lead of the mind, not your emotions. Language is the passport of your mind! "Language is impregnated with individual characteristics of a person."*(John Binge)*

People that are language-savvy get along better with others and communicate their thoughts in a clear-cut way. **You are what you think, and you are what you say!** So, think before saying anything, and be sure to observe the rule:

Only the mind-governed tongue orchestrates the life fun!

*Next, make the development of your **Emotional Intelligence Skills** your main concern in life because uncontrolled emotions generate a lot of unpleasant consequences that we must deal with. Oversee your emotions to call yourself a real gentleman or a lady.*

The emotional goal works for the aristocratism of your soul!

Third, in the Mental Department, living is a life-long learning!

Your intelligence is the basis for your Self-Installation in life. You can establish the connection with the Universal Mind only if you keep developing yours.

Absorb the knowledge, process it for its validity, sort out the redundant mess, and organize your mind into **the compartments of wisdom at hand** that you can tap into at any time to solve any problem. Rely on your intuition and the love-mission.

True love is devoid of frustration and sex-identification!

Forth, in the Spiritual Department, follow God in your intuition intention!

Take care of your soul's health and balance that can be sustained only *if, no matter what, you are Godly in the Godless world!* Have the spiritual, not just religious barometer guiding your inner weather and charging the mental compass of your life.

In my thought, I report only to God!

Fifth, in the Universal Dimension, become One with everything under the Sun!

Develop the **UNIFICATION MENTALITY** with all life on Earth and appreciate every minute of your limited life-time.

To Life-Thrive, Be Joyfully Alive!

Let the Universal Happiness Rein in Your Soul's Domain!

Only in Unity with the Universal Mind
Can We all Survive as the Kind!

3. Your Time is Limited!

(An Inspirational Booster)

I was and I am
A totally irresistible femme/ man!

I dazzle, I puzzle every man, a friend,
And the like on my life's turn pike!

I drive on it consciously and without a frown
I slow up my slow down!

Therefore, in me thought,
I report Only to God!

And I devote my life's mission
To my final to God admission!

"Your Time is Limited,
Don't Limit it, Living Someone's Life!"

(Steve Jobs)

4. The Music of Life

(An Inspirational Booster)

The music of life is the what

Can easily be stopped

      By death at play

      Any minute and any day!

Death trims our pleasant dreams,

And it out-steams crazy emotional whims

      It freezes an unfinished talk

      And stops the final walk

But it will never warn

That you will be gone

      In an unpredictable fraction

      Of the universal time / space action!

Life is going on, and it's worth my having been born!

Life and Death are here at the Same Time.

So, Take a while to Welcome Life with a Smile!

5. Go Beyond the Terrestrial; Be Celestial!

(An Inspirational Booster)

Take a moment to see

Things nobody can foresee!

   Look at the sky and stand in awe

    To the vastness of all!

Feel that you are a part

Of the infinity's Universal Art!

   Unite inside with the stars and the ocean,

  With the Earth and everything that's in motion!

Feel One

With a bird and the Sun,

    Admire the night

    At its every sight!

Appreciate the moment of stillness

And the vastness of relativeness!

   Say, "Thank you!" to the Magic of Life

    That you can help to thrive!

Process in your brain's mine

The DNA of each universal sign!

Read into Those Hazy Shapes;
They are the Language of Our Fates!

6. The State of Inner Bliss is Beyond Happiness!

(An Inspirational Booster)

Think of happiness as the state of inner bliss
That you release

From fear, mental tension, confusion,
And emotional infusion,

All desires and whims
That clutter your psychological ins!

These frantic patterns that we need to crack
Should be all thrown away as an Old Sack!

Removing the toxic mental myths,
We'll acquire wisdom without any ifs!

We'll stop working at our life scene
And start living happily with a spin!

Give a Moment of Love to Everything Here and Above!

Long Live the Belief in Happiness without IF!

7. Radiate Your Personal Stamina!

The Auto-Induction for Self-Production:

I am a Strong, Confident, and Consistent Master of My Firm Will!

I Can, I Want to, and I Will!
I'm Becoming Better and Better with Each Coming Day!

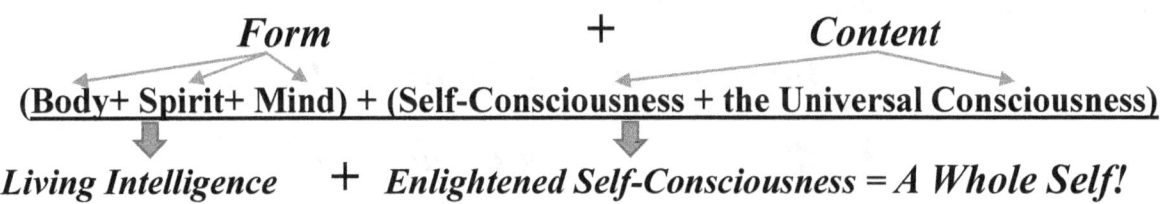

The Image of the Best of Me
is hidden in My Life's FORM+ CONTENT Glee!

8. Be the Living Intelligence in Action!

The Route of Self-Salvation:

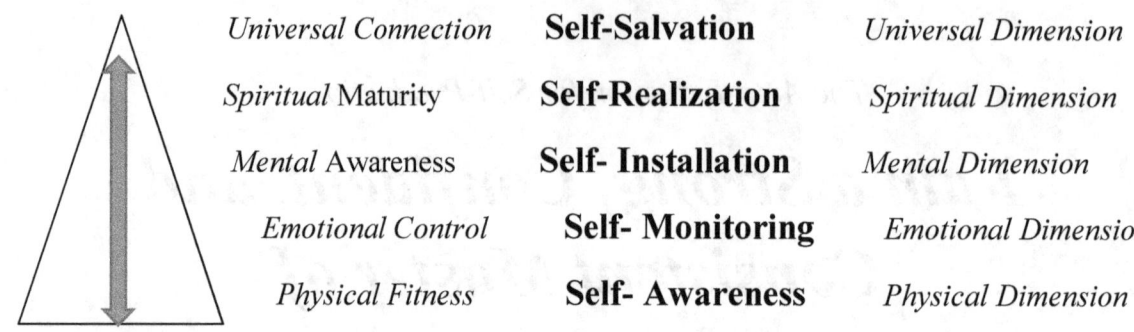

Universal Connection	**Self-Salvation**	*Universal Dimension*
Spiritual Maturity	**Self-Realization**	*Spiritual Dimension*
Mental Awareness	**Self-Installation**	*Mental Dimension*
Emotional Control	**Self-Monitoring**	*Emotional Dimension*
Physical Fitness	**Self-Awareness**	*Physical Dimension*

In conclusion, starting with getting to know yourself better and obtaining ***physical intelligence***, you have learnt to monitor your emotions, control your bad habits, and master ***emotional intelligence***. By intellectualizing your emotion and strengthening aware attention to life, you are rationalizing your life and constantly enriching your general intelligence and life-awareness. On this path, you will build up your ***professional intelligence*** and ensure your ***Self-Installation*** in life. Growing professionally and developing your creative intelligence, you will be raising your ***spiritual intelligence***, accomplishing ***Self-Actualization*** in life that will be becoming much happier and more content.

Body+ Spirit+ Mind + Self-Consciousness + the Universal Consciousness

This process will inevitably be governed by your ***ascending self-consciousness,*** more appreciation of life in the Now, and the unification in spirit with the entire life, getting connected to the ***Universal Intelligence.*** So, finally, you'll be able to auto-suggestively declare:

I Admit - I'm Physically-Fit!

I Admit - I'm Emotionally-Fit!

I Admit - I'm Mentally-Fit!

I Admit - I'm Spiritually-Fit!

I Admit - I'm Universally-Fit!

Self-Salvation is in Soul-Maturation!

9. To Rise Beyond the Skies, Be Overly Wise!

*Don't let your soul repose,
or decompose;
Keep it from decay;*

----

*Make it work
full time,
Night and Day!*

Life in its Universal Form is Our Eternal Uniform!

10. The Final Invocation for the Soul's Reformation!

Let the light of God

Be reflected in my face;

Let the wisdom of God

Be reflected in my mental space!

    Let the accuracy of God

    Be reflected in my speech;

    Let the beauty of God

    Be reflected in my every body's inch!

Let the power of God

Be reflected in my deeds;

Let the love of God

Be reflected in my kids!

    Let the compassion of God

    Be reflected in my attitude;

    Let the passion of God

    Be reflected in my soul's aptitude!

Only then may God

Take me off the sign "Stop!"

And release me into the life stream,

As perfect as His every creation seam!

Carpe Diem! Some Day is Today!

Our Common Salvation is in the Extra-Terrestrial Spiritual Maturation!

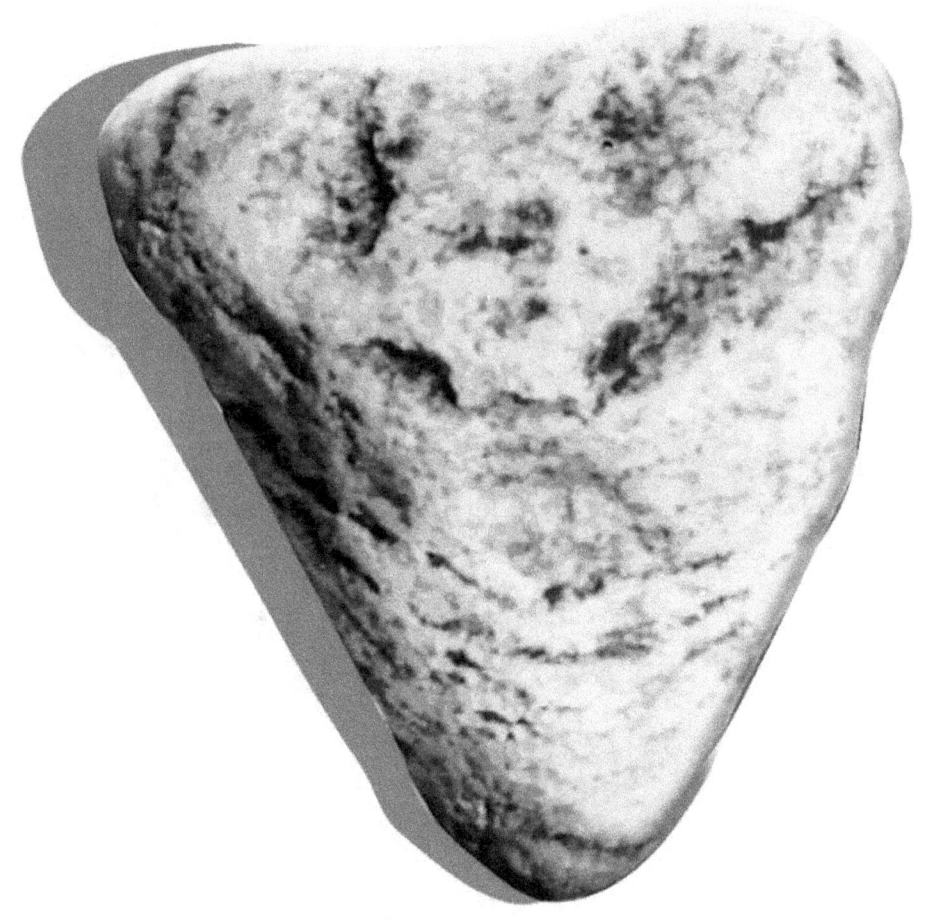

(I am an Alien!)

Don't Be Terrestrially Reactive, Be Extra-Terrestrially Proactive!

Post Thought!

"Go Beyond, Fully Beyond, Completely Beyond!"

If we manage to preserve and revitalize *our bio-energetic health in sync* with developing our *emotional control, spiritualized intelligence,* and *Godly attitude to each other,* we'll raise our self-consciousness and establish the connection with the Universal Mind, overseeing our lives.

You Can Complete Your Life with a Spiritual Zest, Going Beyond the Terrestrial Quest!

Nothing is Impossible if
We Make Our Dreams Irreversible!

The Soul-Installation Track is Not Crowded
For Those who are Holistically-Rounded!

1. "I Have a Dream!"

(Martin Luther King Jr.)

When we arrived in the USA, there were many things that we lacked in the former Soviet Union of those destructive times, but the country of plenty lacked one thing that my 13-year old daughter noticed very soon and told me one day after she came home from Mamaroneck school in Westchester.

"Mom, I know my dream now. I will start a business in this country; ***I will build the center for kids!*** *They have no Pioneer Canters for kids, where I learnt folk-dancing, ballet - dancing, sewing, fishing, swimming, space-flying, and toy-making.* **Poor kids. They don't have that here. Nor do they have anything for teenagers. What should I do here? Where do I go after school?** *My school peers talk only about parties, bars sex, and sleep-overs".*

I was glad that she started thinking in the American way business-wise, but I was truly upset that she was right about the second part of her observation that very soon became a true nightmare for me. The reality changed her dream, and even though she became a computer-designer and got four books for kids published, she did not manage ***to bridge her dream and the reality and become totally self-realized.*** She had never spoken about it again.

Years went by, but I have never forgotten that conversation and the spark in Yolanda's eyes because I saw the same spark in the eyes of many of my students whom I try to inspire to never betray their dreams and become what they aspire to be, not what just secures their life As a matter of fact, ***my five books on self-awareness, self-monitoring, self-installation, self-realization, and self-salvation*** in life, are inspired by my daughter's unrealized dream to have the center like some day here.

My dream is to have ***a free center "JUPITER"*** that will be structured in five rings - ***physical, emotional, mental, spiritual, and universal,*** opening the doors to **FIVE SPACE STATIONS:**

5. Universal / Space Station
4. Spiritual / Space Station
3. Mental / Space Station
2. Emotional Space Station
1. Physical Space Station

The Choices We Make Dictate the Life we Live!

Wouldn't it be great to have the **PSYSICAL SPACE STATION** for the kids and teenagers where they will be developing their physical abilities, like it was in the ancient Greek school for Spartans. They will have a chance to enrich their *cognitive skills* and learn many new interesting things of their choice, as well as train their *digital skills* in the most creative ways. *(the book "I am Free to Be the Best of Me!")*

Next, at the **EMOTIONAL STACE STATION**, the kids will learn about an array of beautiful human emotions and how to handle their Amygdala gland with the help of the best movies, tales, works of art, and beautiful classic music There will be instructors – *psychologists- emotionalists and robot-friends* to back them up if they happen to swoon emotionally. *(the book "Soul-Refining")*

The holistic pyramid of essential *Vistas of Intelligence* will be at their fingerprints when they chose to spiral up to the **MENTAL SPACE STATION** to fill up the gaps in the levels of intelligence that this book features. They will enhance their awareness by connecting their two brains and boosting their creativity and ascertaining their dream of what they want to become *(the book "Living Intelligence or the Art of Becoming!")*

The most inspiring knowledge of the human evolutionary *spiritual growth* will await them at the **SPIRITUAL SPACE STATION,** with no preaching or religious indoctrination, but insightful, interesting enlightening the minds to shape their *spiritualized intelligence.(the book "Self-Taming!")*

The space-time journey into the impossible will complete at the **UNIVERSAL SPACE STATION,** with breath-taking make-belief flight of imagination in *the top observatory + a virtual space* station that will take them on interstellar travels into space. *(the book "Beyond the Terrestrial!)*

And the best thing of all - there will be no obligations, no words: "***You are supposed to…"/ "You need to pay first!" That's not your station! "You need to first do this…"***

The possibilities are limitless, as well as our incredible NOW that is, in fact, our wonderous future!

Start Radiating the Inner Bliss of Your Everyday Happiness Release!

LONG LIVE THE BEAT OF SO BE IT!

Dr. Ray with Her Inspirational Say:

1. *"Emotional Diplomacy or Follow the Bliss of the Uncatchable Is!"/ Editorial LEIRIS, New York, USA, 2010*

2. *"Four Dimensions of a Soul" (Auto-Suggestive Psychology in Russian) / LEIRIS Publishing, New York, USA, 2011*

3. *"Americanize Your Language, Emotionalize Your Speech!" / Nova Press, USA, 2011*

4. *"It Too Shall Pass!" (Inspirational Boosters in Four Dimensions) / Xlibris, 2012*

5. *"I am Strong in My Spirit!" (Inspirational Boosters in Russian) / Xlibris, 20135.*

6. *"Language Intelligence or Universal English" (Method of the Right Language Behavior), Book One / Xlibris, 2013*

7. *"Language Intelligence or Universal English" (Remedy Your Language Habits," Book Two / Xlibris, 2013*

8. *"Language Intelligence or Universal English," (Remedy Your Speech Skills) Book Three / Xlibris, 2013*

9. *"Living Intelligence or the Art of Becoming" (A New Paradigm of Self-Creation) Xlibris, 2015*

10. *"My Solar System," (Auto-Suggestive Psychology for Inner Ecology) Xlibris, 2015*

11. *Beyond the Terrestrial! (Be the Station for Self-Inspiration!), Xlibris, June 2016*

12. *Soul-Refining! (Toplinkpublishing.com. May 2017)*

13. *"I Am Free to Be the Best of Me!*

14. *"Self-Taming!"(Book Whip Publishing, 2018)*

----

www. Language – fitness.com / Emotional Diplomacy.com

- rimma143@hotmail.com / Tel. (203) 212-2673

www.ingramcontent.com/pod-product-compliance
Lightning Source LLC
Chambersburg PA
CBHW051752100526
44591CB00017B/2665